"Joe Burns has written an import. ries of examples the importance of the strike to the past and future of the labor movement. Burns shows how the strike has been reduced to near death by the constant hostility of the courts, the union busting tactics of management, and the incompetence and cowardice of union leaders. Burns also makes an eloquent plea for a return to old fashioned, class conscious, militant unionism which, he argues persuasively, can restore the strike and rejuvenate the labor movement."—Julius Getman, author of *Restoring the Power of Unions: It Takes a Movement*

"A close look at labor history reveals that strikes have not only been a critical vehicle of workers' power but have also been an irreplaceable fulcrum of workers' transformation. It's been in strikes that skilled and unskilled workers, white workers and workers of color, men and women, and native born and immigrant workers have discovered, experienced, and acted upon their shared interests. It's been in strikes that capitalism's tensions between competition and cooperation have been played out, that workers have experienced the meaning of solidarity and the prospects for a future society based on it. The disappearance of the strike, so well explained here by Joe Burns, is not only a consequence of labor's weakness; it is a cause of it, too."—Peter Rachleff, author of *Hard-Pressed in the Heartland: The Hormel Strike and the Future of the Labor Movement*

"Joe Burns shows us how badly employers needed to outlaw solidarity—and the drastic consequences for workers. He argues that unions cannot combat the corporate onslaught with 'high road' rhetoric or symbolic actions; they must exercise their power to disrupt the business as usual of profit-making. This book will prompt some major rethinking."—Jane Slaughter, founder of *Labor Notes Magazine*

REVIVING THE STRIKE

REVIVING THE STRIKE

HOW WORKING PEOPLE CAN REGAIN
POWER AND TRANSFORM AMERICA

JOE BURNS

PUBLISHING

BROOKLYN, NEW YORK

Printed in the United States of America
10 9 8 7 6 5 4 3 2

Ig Publishing
392 Clinton Avenue
Brooklyn, NY 11238
www.igpub.com

Library of Congress Cataloging-in-Publication Data

Burns, Joe.
Reviving the strike : how working people can regain power and transform America / Joe Burns.
    p. cm.
  ISBN 978-1-935439-24-0 (pbk.)
  1. Strikes and lockouts--United States. 2. Civil disobedience--Unit-
ed States. 3. Collective bargaining--United States. I. Title.
  HD5324.B817 2011
  331.892'973--dc22
                                    2011014363

To Betty Burns

CONTENTS

1. THE STRIKE AND THE RISE OF THE WORKING CLASS

By wielding the threat of a powerful, production-halting strike, trade unionists forged a better way of life for millions of working class Americans during the roughly fifty year period from 1930 through 1980. During this time, workers secured real wage increases, pensions, employer-paid health care, protection from arbitrary treatment by supervisors, as well as seniority systems that rewarded length of time with the employer. Writing in 1962, labor economist Albert Rees declared the strike "by far the most important source of union power."[1]

Rees was not alone in this belief. Reviewing labor textbooks publishing from the 1950s through the 1980s, one finds near universal agreement that collective bargaining made little sense unless it was backed by the threat of a strike that halted production. In his 1980 book *Labor Economics*, Roy Helfgott wrote that, "the union's ability to strike, and thus halt the employer's production, is essential to the collective bargaining process. In this view it is the potential of a disruption in production that induces employers to strive to effectuate agreement with the union."[2] Writing nearly a quarter of a century earlier, labor analyst Jack Barbash made largely the same point in the 1956 book *The Practice of Unionism*, stating that "The decisive weapons which the unions utilize (or hold in reserve) to give meaning to collective bargaining are the strike, the boycott, and the picket line....There can be no collective bargaining, if, from the union's standpoint it cannot utilize these means."[3]

Most workers of the period did not need textbooks to tell them all this, as they knew about the power of the strike from their own experiences. During the 1950s, for example, workers repeatedly struck to back up their bargaining demands. Major strikes (those of over 1000 workers) averaged 350 per year during the decade, as opposed to 20 per year from 2000 through 2009.[4] Unions of the 1950s shut down entire industries for weeks or even months at a time to win improvements for their members.

One can pick an industry and see how the strike made a difference in the lives of workers. Take auto, for example. In the early 1930s, life was difficult for autoworkers. Although the pay was higher than for other manufacturing work, the job was sporadic and stressful.[5] An autoworker could be employed one week, and then have to get by without a paycheck the next. In addition, autoworkers were required to work off the clock, cutting their hourly pay considerably, and auto companies often targeted workers over forty for termination, considering them past their prime. Autoworkers also faced the speedup, the ever-increasing pace of production work.

By the mid-1950s, however, the auto industry had undergone a major transformation. No longer a high turnover job, auto work became the ticket to a better life. With the job now came employer provided health care, pensions, and supplemental unemployment insurance. Although still suffering from the monotony inherent in production work, many workers could afford a home and to send their kids to college. Twenty years of hardnosed collective bargaining, backed by strike activity, had wrestled these improvements from the reluctant management of auto companies.

Autoworkers also joined with workers in other industries to gain concessions from employers. During the great strike wave of 1946, for example, autoworkers joined steelworkers, miners, and hundreds of thousands of workers in other industries in engaging in long-term strikes. At General Motors, the UAW struck for 113 days, shutting down 80 plants around the country, and eventually winning an 18.5 cent per hour wage increase as a result.[6] In 1949, by threatening a repeat of the 1946 strike, the UAW forced Ford to agree to an employer-funded pension plan. It took a 104-day strike to make Chrysler see the light and agree to fully fund pensions in advance.[7] In 1955, the union fought for a guaranteed annual wage. With a $125 million strike fund in hand, the UAW again targeted Ford, eventually winning supplemental unemployment benefits to address the lack of year-round employment.

In industry after industry, the power of the strike transformed the lives of countless numbers of working class Americans during the middle of the twentieth century. Truck drivers, grocery workers, carpenters and steelworkers all improved their working conditions through collective bargaining backed by a strike. Historian Jack Metzgar, the son of a steelworker, describes how the strike changed his family's life:

> From the time my father joined the union in 1936 until the 1959 strike, the average real wage of steelworkers increased 110 percent, with the bulk of the increase coming after the war. Think of that a minute. Think what it does for a family's well-being to have more real spending power year after year, to experience a steady relentless improvement in its standard of living for more than two decades."[8]

However, such improvements did not come easily. "Through ten sets of negotiations and five strikes from 1946 to 1956," Metzger recalled, "the steel companies fought every advance the union sought—and did so in a highly public way."[9]

A BRIEF HISTORY OF THE STRIKE

For most of the history of the United States, the strike has been the main weapon for working people seeking to improve their conditions of employment. There have been an estimated 300,000 strikes throughout U.S. history,[10] with some of the earliest ones involving craft workers who were trying to defend their individual trades against a rising system of capitalism that was transforming independent artisans into wage-earning employees.[11] These strikes encountered hostility from the judicial system, which considered such efforts to be a restraint of trade. Yet even in the face of government repression, workers persevered, forming national labor organizations to give form and structure to their strike efforts.

As the capitalist economy expanded throughout the nineteenth century, workers continued to strike in a variety of different ways. Sometimes, the strike took the form of a refusal of skilled workers to work for a particular employer who failed to pay fair wages, while at other times the strike involved the targeting of an entire local industry. With the rise of massive corporations in the late 1800s, some strikes, particularly in rail, turned into nationwide confrontations between labor and capital. Not simply labor-management disputes, such strikes expanded into community uprisings against an economy increasingly controlled by a privileged few.

From the late 1800s through the 1920s, the dominant form of trade unionism in the United States was craft unionism. The economic basis of craft unionism was control over the supply of labor. Craft unions, comprised of highly skilled workers, could often win strikes merely by withholding their labor, as employers could not replace them with lesser skilled workers. By limiting entry into a trade through union rules or control of training, craft unions could drive up the cost of union labor through simple supply and demand. The modern, popular conception of the strike comes largely from the actions of craft unionists, namely the concerted refusal to work until employee demands are met.

The fatal flaw of craft unionism, however, was that it was built upon the politics of exclusion. By limiting entrance into a trade, craft unionism protected the wages of union members at the cost of excluding other workers. Rather than reach out to all workers, for example, craft unions restricted membership to white, mostly native-born skilled workers. Craft unionism thus represented the solidarity of white labor. The limited and exclusionary nature of solidarity practiced by craft unions constituted one of the major weaknesses of the labor movement during this period.

Over time, changes in technology, the introduction of mass production techniques, and the deskilling of labor rendered a strike based on merely withholding labor ineffective. Since the union no longer controlled the labor supply, it became simple for employers to find replacements to take striking workers' jobs. Therefore, for the vast majority of workers, most of whom were not members of craft unions, a different kind of strike was required. This need for a new type of unionism would find its voice in the industrial union movement of the 1930s.

In the decades leading up to the 1930s, progressive union activists were among the leading proponents of industrial unionism. Opposed to the narrowness and exclusion of craft unionism, advocates of industrial unionism argued that all workers in an industry needed to unite and strike together. The result was some of the greatest strikes in American history. From future Socialist Party leader Eugene Debs leading the Pullman railway strike of 1894 to the 1910s strike wave led by the Industrial Workers of the World, progressive labor activists repeatedly attempted to break free of the constraints of craft unionism to establish a form of unionism that would benefit all workers.

However, despite the valiant efforts of these progressives, by the early 1930s the labor movement was on the ropes. During the 1920s, a combination of trade union conservatism and government repression had decimated unions, driving many leftists out of the labor movement. Thus, the heart of the new industrial economy—the massive industrial concerns in manufacturing such as auto and steel—remained unorganized.

Then, out of the depths of the Great Depression, trade unionists developed a new kind of unionism based on a powerful, production-halting strike. Despite unemployment in the double digits, workers struck repeatedly and successfully during the 1930s. The success of strikes during this period can be explained by a number of factors. First, in contrast to the narrow craft unionism of previous decades, striking industrial unions united all workers at an employer or within an industry. Second, strikers employed aggressive tactics to stop production at a struck employer, such as mass picketing or sit-down strikes, ensuring that workers were not replaced by scabs. Finally, solidarity ensured that workers were not striking alone. This powerful strike transformed the labor movement and laid the basis for decades of relative prosperity for working people. I refer to this form of strike activity as the "traditional strike," to distinguish it from the weak, modern version of the strike employed by trade unionists since the 1980s.

After World War II, with pent up wage demands, strike activity exploded across the nation. Unlike in the 1930s, strikes following World War II were no longer battles to the death between employees and employers. Instead, with labor's victories of the 1930s still fresh and corporate profits relatively healthy, most employers sought to outlast striking workers rather than crush strikes outright. Strikes thus became routine affairs in which plants were typically shut down in an orderly fashion prior to the strike.

The period between the end of World War II and 1980

represents the height of the traditional strike. Through collective bargaining, unions won pensions, employer paid health care and sharply rising real wages. With hundreds of thousands of workers striking at once, unions were able to build industry-wide agreements. Yet, during this period of labor prosperity, the seeds of eventual union destruction were being planted. On the legal front, the industry-wide tactics of solidarity, so essential to the traditional strike, were outlawed by Congress in the 1940s and 1950s. In addition, with employers simply shutting down production in the face of the strike, unions no longer needed the militant mass picketing and dramatic tactics that had been the key sources of union power in the 1930s. Such tactics came to be considered relics of the past, rather than essential elements of successful striking. Thus, when the anti-union employer assault intensified in the 1980s, unions had already been disarmed.

As a result, the strike employed in the 1980s and beyond differed fundamentally from the traditional strike that had come before it. Instead of engaging in solidarity and production-halting tactics, most unions merely set up picket lines and then watched as scabs walked past them to take striking worker's jobs. For the first time in U.S. labor history, strike strategy was not based on halting the production of the employer. While many chose to blame union impotence, economic trends or more aggressive employers, the real problem was the abandonment of traditional strike tactics and philosophy.

THE ABANDONMENT OF THE STRIKE

During the 1980s, it became fashionable on both the left and the right of the labor movement to view the post-World War II period as a happy social accord between labor and capital. Certainly, on the surface, this viewpoint was understandable, as in many industries, unions and management developed cozy relationships, with employers even loaning money to unions on occasion when their strike funds diminished.

However, with the benefit of hindsight, the idea of a social accord has rightfully been challenged. We can now see it was more of a temporary truce. As labor historian Nelson Lichtenstein notes, "During the first two decades after World War II few unionists could have been found to declare that their relationship with corporate America particularly agreeable or stable. Most would have thought the very idea of a 'social compact' between themselves and their corporate adversaries a clever piece of management propaganda."[12] Such an accord, according to Lichtenstein, was less a social compact than a "dictate imposed upon an all-too-reluctant labor movement in an era of its political retreat and internal division."[13]

Today, that retreat is complete, and the labor movement no longer makes use of a production-halting strike, or, for the most part, any type of strike at all. The statistics are clear: workers are striking at a miniscule fraction of the rate that they did in previous decades. In 1952, there were 470 major strikes (those of more than 1000 workers) involving 2,746,000 workers. By contrast, in 2008, there were only 15 major work stoppages, involving 72,000 workers.[14] Strikes nowadays are also much shorter than strikes of the past. In 1952, almost 49 million days were lost to work stoppages; in 2008, the number of days lost was starkly lower—less than 2 million. The time lost striking represented .38 percent of all work time in 1952, compared to a miniscule .01 percent of all work time in 2008.

Its not just major strikes that are disappearing. While the Reagan administration stopped keeping data on strikes of fewer than 1,000 workers in 1981, Joseph McCartin of Georgetown University, who has extensively studied strike activity, believes that "there is little reason to believe that smaller scale work stoppages defied the downward trend in major work stoppages."[15] McCartin notes that workers in smaller strikes are more vulnerable to being permanently replaced, so the downward trend in smaller strikes would likely be similar to that of major ones.

The abandonment of the strike has led to the erosion of the wage, retirement, and health care gains of the postwar period. For example, real weekly wages dropped from an average of $315.44 in 1972 to $274.49 in 2006, using 1982 dollars as the baseline.[16] Workers also have to put in more hours on the job per week to earn that lower weekly wage. There has also been a massive shift in the costs of health care from the employer to the employee. Whereas two decades ago, most union contracts contained employer-provided health care with minimal employee contributions, high deductibles and premiums are now the norm. In addition, the defined-benefit pension, once a staple of trade union contracts, has become an endangered species. According to the Employee Benefits Research Institute, 84 percent of active workers who had a retirement plan participated in a defined benefit pension plan in 1979.[17] By 2003, that number had dropped to 37 percent.

With the decline of the strike, employers have been able to aggressively attack work rules and the quality of work life. A major component of the war on labor of the last few decades has been a drive for greater productivity. In other words, more work for the same pay. One example of this is in the auto industry, where the "lean production" methods of the early 1990s decreased the idle time for autoworkers at one plant from fifteen seconds a minute to a mind-numbing three seconds per minute.[18] Working at this kind of speed leads to more stress on the job and a greater chance of employee injury.

The disappearance of the strike should prompt much soul searching within the labor movement. Yet, there has been remarkably little discussion over the loss of what was once considered to be the main source of union power. As AFL-CIO President Richard Trumka said unequivocally in the early 1990s, unions need "their only true weapon—the right to strike. Without that weapon, organized labor in America will soon cease to exist."[19]

Why then has the strike virtually disappeared? The short answer is that today's "strike" has lost two of the key components that defined the powerful strike upon which the modern labor movement was built: the halting of production, and an industry-wide approach to standardizing wages, i.e. worker solidarity. These components, which represent the main differences between the powerful, effective traditional strike and the weak, ineffective modern strike, are the necessary starting point for any discussion of trade union renewal.

THE ECONOMICS OF STOPPING PRODUCTION

To traditional trade unionists, the point of a strike was to make an employer's pocketbook bleed. In their eyes, a successful strike must stop production or otherwise inflict sufficient economic harm to force an employer to agree to union demands. That simple, commonsense notion formed the basis of labor economics for the first one hundred fifty odd years of American trade unionism. By the 1980s, however, trade unionists had abandoned this philosophy in favor of a management-inspired view of striking. That, more than anything else, explains the weakness of the modern union movement.

Today, the prevailing view of a strike is one of workers withholding their labor in order to pressure an employer to reach an agreement. In this conception of a strike, strikers force the market to determine the value of their labor as a group by withdrawing their services. The alternative view, held by trade unionists of the middle part of the twentieth century, viewed a strike as workers halting production in order to force the employer to agree to union demands. Understanding these very different conceptions of striking is vital to labor's revival.

According to the "free market" view of management, labor is simply a commodity—nothing more, nothing less. A commodity is an object traded in the marketplace without regard to its origin. Commodities such as lumber or oil constitute inputs into the production process. Commodities are things. To employers, human labor is no different than any other input into production—mere objects to be used up. Thus, according to management economists, if a worker in a non-union shop wants a raise, he or she would go to their manager and request one. If the manager believed that the company could purchase another worker's labor more cheaply, the manager would refuse the worker's wage demand. The worker could then either remain on the job at his or her current salary, or quit. According to this view, just like any other supplier in the production process, the worker has the "freedom" to take their productive power elsewhere for a better price, if available.

Traditional trade unionists rejected this scenario for two reasons. The first being that the bargaining power between workers and employers is not equal, as a worker has little ability to influence the wages that a company pays. In this case, any kind of bargaining turns out to be a sham, as the employee is forced to work for wages set by the employer. The other reason is that workers are not raw materials such as lumber or oil—they are people, with rights and needs unrelated to the price an employer is willing to pay for their labor.

Today's strike, unfortunately, represents a fundamentally "free market" approach. For any given group of workers who threaten to strike for a raise after the expiration of their contract, management can either meet the workers' wage demands or refuse them, prompting a strike. However, under current labor law, the employer is then permitted to hire permanent replacement scabs to replace the striking workers. The success of the strike depends solely on whether or not the employer is able to replace the striking workers. This is precisely why the modern version of the strike is so ineffective. A strike which involves putting up picket lines and waiting for scabs to cross while workers essentially "quit" en masse is not one that favors workers in any way. But since current legal rules on striking force most workers to leave their jobs with a high degree of certainty that scabs will replace them, workers are ultimately faced with the choice of either accepting the employer's offer or losing their jobs. And while labor law does provide that the workers in a failed strike must be offered their jobs back when the strike is over—as the strikers are not technically fired—this is cold comfort to anyone who is forced to spend time without a paycheck. Given the type of anti-labor economics in play here, there should be no surprise at the drastic decline in strike activity in recent decades.

Now, certainly, it is of value to an employer not to have to replace an entire group of workers, so companies do have some incentive to make a deal as long as labor costs don't rise too much. And, in certain industries, a company may not want the bad press associated with a strike and thus be willing to grant a small wage premium. In other situations, the workforce may be larger and/or more skilled, like the craft unions of old; in these cases, collective bargaining can have some impact. For example, highly skilled workers in certain circumstances, such as the 27,000 machinists at Boeing in 2008, are able to carry off traditional strikes. However, even in those kinds of situations, highly skilled workers have been replaced when their demands were higher than what the employer was willing to pay.

Overall, however, the management-oriented version of striking simply does not work for workers on a widespread basis. In very few labor markets can strikers make serious gains by merely withholding labor, as management can easily hire scabs to replace all but the most highly skilled workers. Traditional trade unionists understood this economic reality and developed effective strike tactics, which focused on stopping the production of the employer. The tactics they used to do this included mass picketing to block plant gates, monopolizing union labor through the closed shop or control of training, the social ostracizing and punishment of scabs, and during a brief but crucial period in the late 1930s, the sit-down strike. Other union tactics, such as secondary strikes and boycotts, were geared towards interrupting the distribution or supply chain of the employer. While the tactics varied, the concept was the same—a strike needed to economically impact an employer. While today's trade unionists assume that labor cannot engage in these types of strike tactics, the labor movement of the past viewed them as legitimate, and routinely denounced judges and politicians who derided such tactics.

As much as one may hate to quote right-wing economists, in many regards they have a better grasp of trade union economics than many trade unionists today. In a book written during the 1980s, *Power and Privilege: Labor Unions in America,* conservative economist Morgan Reynolds describes the reasons that unions must stop production:

> A union's problem is painfully obvious: organized strikers must shut down the enterprise, close the market to everyone else—uncooperative workers, union members, disenchanted former strikers, and employers—in order to force wages and working conditions above free-market rates....Unions must actively interfere with freedom of trade in labor markets in order to deliver on their promises.[20]

Reynolds goes on to state that "wages and working conditions above free-market results can be preserved only by force or threat of force."[21] If one sets aside the free market jargon, this is a good argument for why unions must stop production, as any other path is just not economically feasible.

According to Reynolds' viewpoint, and the viewpoint of corporations in general, workers are nothing more than inputs into the production process, no different from lumber or machine parts. Now, as a statement of fact, an employer does indeed purchase the capacity of an individual to work for a given period of time, like any other commodity. Yet the labor movement long resisted treating the sale of labor by the same rules as commodities, believing instead that workers had rights unrelated to the price an employer paid for their labor. In turn, workers believed they had rights in the factories their labor created. As one sit-down striker at a General Motors plant in Flint, Michigan during the 1930s explained in justifying the strike he was taking part in, "Our hides are wrapped around those machines."[22] The traditional vehemence against scabs stems from this underlying belief that they were stealing workers' jobs.

In labor textbooks from the 1950s through the 1980s, it was taken for granted that the purpose of a strike was to stop production. Thus, Roy Helfgott wrote in *Labor Economics* that "The objective of any strike, of course, is to halt the employer's operation, thus causing a loss to him that he may come to recognize as being greater than the benefit of resisting the union's demands."[23] Until the mid-1980s, through numerous editions, *The Practice of Collective Bargaining* was a standard textbook in labor economics. The authors, James Begin and Edwin Beal, were both university economists, and clearly understood the purpose of striking:

> The immediate strike objective of the industrial union in manufacturing is to control physical access to the workplace. This denies the employer the use of a productive plant until it is ransomed by a satisfactory settlement.... The underlying strategy in all of them is to prevent the replacement of strikers of many varieties and degrees of

semiskill by other individuals who can be taught strikers' jobs."[24]

Begin and Beal also noted the traditional point of the picket line:

"Picketing the plant is not a siege, it is a blockade. It cuts the plant off from a vital element of production: labor. It defends the approaches to the plant against the entrance of people who might provide the labor. Who are these people who might want to go in the open gate? Anybody and everybody, including union members who weaken."[25]

This conception of a strike and the purpose of the picket line is very different from the one held by today's labor movement. To the traditional trade unionist of the 1940s and 1950s, the idea that an employer should continue production during a strike was considered antithetical to the goals of the labor movement. By the 1980s, however, conventional wisdom had reversed, and stopping production had become a fringe idea.

THE ECONOMICS OF SOLIDARITY

From the earliest days of the union movement in the United States, workers understood the need to unite with other workers in their industry to seek common standards. As labor economist Bruce Kaufman summarized, "If unions can organize all competing firms, they can use collective bargaining to establish uniform labor costs across the industry ...and thus take wages out of competition...."[26] This understanding was central to the development of trade unionism.

The reason unions need to standardize wages across an industry is simple economics. If workers at one company win a wage increase, that company would then be undercut by other companies in the same industry that are paying their workers a lesser wage. Eventually, if an employer's competitors are not forced to match wages, the unionized employer will lose market share to its lower wage paying competitors. Why would an employer agree to contract terms raising its labor costs if its competitors are not being forced to similarly agree to increases?

The failure to organize an entire industry historically weakened unions and undermined collective bargaining agreements, as well as upsetting employers. Historian Phillip Taft has recounted employer complaints against the union of iron molders in the 1860s for failing to organize the entire industry. "One of the sources of differences between the employers and the union," Taft writes, "was the failure of the union to raise prices in the eastern shops so as to equalize costs between eastern and western producers."[27] In fact, the earliest regional and national trade unions were formed to standardize wages in an industry. As historian John Commons notes, "In the field of trade unionism the nationalization of the market gave birth to the national trade union."[28] Commons writes how, in the 1860s, stove molders began producing in competing markets

> In order that union conditions should be maintained even in the best organized centers, it then became imperatively necessary to equalize competitive conditions in the various localities. That led to a well-knit national organization to control working conditions, trade rules and strikes.[29]

As Lloyd Ulman indicates in *The Rise of National Trade Unions*, the internal development of unions was guided by efforts to contend with changing labor and product markets.[30] Traditional unions thus formed on the local and national level to achieve wage standardization.

In recent decades, in the face of an employer onslaught and a legal system constructed to prevent wage standardization, trade unions have abandoned the traditional goal of wage standardization within industries. In previous generations, for example, autoworkers all joined the same union so that workers at one automaker would not be able to undercut other workers at another company. However, in the modern period, locals of the same international union negotiate different pay scales, even at the same corporation.

THE WRATH AGAINST PUBLIC SECTOR UNIONISM

The contemporary labor movement is exactly what one would expect to find in the absence of a production-halting strike, namely, a weak movement forced to rely on government assistance to survive. In fact, the labor movement is increasingly concentrated in the public sector, as the percentage of union members in the public sector increased from 34.4 percent in 1983 to 48.9 percent in 2008.[31] And in 2009, for the first time, a majority of union members were public employees.

While public sector workers need and deserve unions, public sector unionism must rest on a bedrock of private sector union strength. Otherwise, as the pay and benefits of private sector workers decrease, attacks on public sector union wages and benefits will increase. Public sector unions will be portrayed as receiving benefits denied to other workers, fostering divisions in the working class. As we have seen over the past few years, in the midst of the greatest economic crisis since the Great Depression, public employees are finding themselves increasingly under attack for these very reasons.

At the same time, many sections of private sector unionism are forced to rely on government intervention. Thus, the building trades focus on lobbying for government projects, which represents a form of public subsidization of their wages. In low wage industries, living wage campaigns attempt to force employers who contract with the government to pay higher wages. Other industries, such as auto, have also required government subsidies. Overall, private sector unions are facing incredible pressure from non-union competitors. Lacking an effective strike and a means to force industry-wide standards, unions are under pressure to bring their labor costs in line with their non-union competitors. The end result are concessions, two tier agreements, and union acceptance of subcontracting. This does not represent a sustainable basis for trade unionism.

With only a minority of workers benefiting from collective bargaining, union workers today are becoming increasingly isolated within the working class. Those who fight to retain their historical benefits are attacked for having benefits that other workers lack. For the majority of union members now in the public sector, union wages and benefits are derided as special privileges at the expense of taxpayers. A 2010 Pew poll found that only 41 percent of Americans have a favorable impression of unions.[32]

Ultimately, the key question facing trade unionists is how to establish new forms of unionism that offer improvements for all workers, not just public employees. For only a labor movement based on independent economic power can survive in the long run. Yet, the contemporary labor movement has instead focused on initiatives which fail to address the essentials of union power. Strategies such as organizing the unorganized and community campaigns, while necessary, fail to address the main economic concerns that must be at the center of union strategy. Independent trade unionism requires a powerful strike, based on solidarity and stopping production. Redeveloping such a strike, while admittedly difficult, must be labor's top priority.

2. THE TURBULENT 1930S: TRADITIONAL TACTICS AND THE RISE OF THE MODERN LABOR MOVEMENT

With the future of the labor movement very much in doubt these days, it is imperative that trade unionists take a look back. Not out of nostalgia, or to romanticize past victories, but to rediscover what a real strike looks like. In particular, labor's victories during the 1930s deserve special scrutiny, given that the two elements necessary for an effective strike—the ability to stop production and worker solidarity—came together during this time to produce a powerful union movement. Charles Craypo, author of the *Economics of Collective Bargaining*, sums it up succinctly, writing about how "union ability to make an employer pay higher labor costs depends essentially on two factors—the extent of worker organization and the ability to stop production."[1] In this chapter, we will examine these two factors in detail, showing how they became so dominant during the 1930s, and why they need to be resurrected if the effective strike—and the labor movement as whole—are to be revitalized.

WORKER RESISTANCE AND THE PRODUCTION-HALTING STRIKE

During the nineteenth century, the dominant form of unionism was craft unionism. Due to the skill of the workers involved, craft unions could stop production by merely withdrawing their labor. In addition, by control of entrance and training to certain skilled trades, craft unions were able to stop employers from hiring non-union labor.[2] Over time, the de-skilling of many trades undermined the power of the craft unions. Employers also sponsored trade schools to diminish the ability of unions to control the supply of labor.[3] As a result of these changes, by the early years of the twentieth century, trade unionists needed to employ different tactics to achieve their aims. Thus, the mass picket line and the sit-down strike were born.

Because of the fierce resistance of management to these new tactics, labor conflicts of the first half of the twentieth century often turned violent. As Phillip Taft and Phillip Ross note in one of the few comprehensive studies on violence in labor history, "The precipitating causes [of violence] have been attempts by pickets and sympathizers to prevent a plant from being reopened with strikebreakers, or attempts of company guards, police, or even by National Guardsmen to prevent such interference."[4] During the great Homestead Steel strike of 1892, 10,000 striking steelworkers and supporters lined the riverbanks leading into Pittsburgh and engaged in a fierce battle with an army of Pinkerton agents attempting to invade the town to start production.[5] Similarly, during the great national rail strikes of 1877, 1886, 1894 and 1922, workers blocked train tracks and prevented trains from running.[6] The "mine wars" of the late nineteenth and early twentieth century were so named because of the intensity of the conflicts.

In *Strike Breaking and Intimidation*, Stephen Norwood describes how the streetcar strikes of the early twentieth century turned many American cities into virtual war zones, complete with "a new form of guerilla warfare, with hand-to-hand combat, night raids, cavalry charges, fighting from rooftops and behind barricades, and retreats in which the wounded were evacuated under heavy cover."[7] This sort of conflict between strikers and strikebreakers was common in industries that employed semi-skilled or unskilled labor, as workers who tried to cross picket lines were deemed scabs, and were often subject to violent reprisals.

Regardless of the particular tactics employed, however, trade unionists of this time understood that to be successful, a strike must economically harm the employer. Because of this, the picket line of the nineteenth and early twentieth century was not a weak form of moral witness, but rather a means to bring real economic pressure to bear on the enemy, i.e. the employer. Even when strikers did not physically prevent the plant from operating, unions employed tactics designed to economically impact the employer. For example, even if an employer was able to continue production during a strike, the use of a labor boycott often nullified this advantage because no one would buy the goods or patronize an establishment that sold struck goods.

In many ways, the labor movement of the first part of the last century faced many of the same conditions workers face today. When the movement made big gains in organizing during the height of the Great Depression, unemployment was in the double digits. There was thus no shortage of workers willing to replace striking workers. Nor was solidarity so strong that desperate workers would not cross picket lines to take other worker's jobs. However, the key difference was that the labor movement back then understood that it needed to stop production in order to win a strike. This is exactly why unions employed dramatic tactics such as mass picketing to shut down the plants, or sit-down strikes. Writing in the 1970s, economists James Robinson and Roger Walker explained why unions in the 1930s had to stop production to be successful:

> Frequently because no alternative sources of skilled labor existed, the craft union did not even have to picket the struck employer. By contrast, many industrial unions were engaged in organizing workers who possessed little

or no identifiable skill. As a result some technique had to be developed to effectively stop employers from replacing striking workers with unemployed laborers who were also unskilled.... However, particularly in the early days of the CIO, local law enforcement authorities frequently were prepared to support employer efforts to smash picket lines. Thus, the strike weapon often was simply not effective. The sit-down strike carried conventional strike activity one step further.[8]

In many ways physical resistance was the only means available to unions of the 1930s to stop production, particularly in the face of aggressive management tactics. Because no other type of strike activity offered any hope of success, trade unionists had no choice but to wage battle against police and company thugs on picket lines.

The height of worker resistance occurred in 1934, when a series of militant strikes swept the nation: the Auto-Light strike in Toledo, the Teamsters truckers strike in Minneapolis, the West Coast long shore strike, and the great nationwide textile strike. In each of these struggles, workers physically prevented production by utilizing a variety of different tactics.[9] During the Toledo Auto-Light strike, a crowd of 10,000, including many supporters from the ranks of the unemployed, broke into the plant and battled hand-to-hand to force the company, which had hired 1500 scabs, to stop production.[10] Even when the National Guard was called out the next day and killed two strikers, the union kept up the pressure, attacking the plant again. The striking workers understood that if the company were allowed to restart production with scabs, the strike would be crushed.

During the great textile strike, "flying squadrons" went from mill to mill, forcing owners to shut down and suspend production. Although the squadrons were mainly non-violent, "the characterization of the squadrons as 'peaceful picketing' misses entirely their character as extralegal enforcers of justice. Swiftly, militantly, the squadrons were not only picketing but forcing the closing of mills."[11] During the 1934 Teamsters strike, any truck that attempted to move goods into the Twin Cities was stopped at a union blockade, where it was met by picketers.[12] Union pickets also waged a fierce battle against police and business owners organized through the Citizen's League. Historian Irving Bernstein describes a key battle of the strike, dubbed the "Battle of Deputies Run":

> The pickets, more numerous and better armed with clubs, baseball bats and pipe, won control of the market place within an hour. The fighting then spread over the city as the pickets pursued the disintegrating police and Citizens' Army remnants. Sporadic outbreaks took place until late evening. The battle had been a complete and decisive victory for the union. No trucks dared to move. The union had taken control not only of the market but also of the streets of Minneapolis. That night, it was said, traffic was directed downtown by pickets rather than policeman."[13]

Although there is a lot more to the story, the essence of the conflict was over whether employers would be allowed to move goods using scabs. The union decisively answered "no" and was able to win the strike, paving the way for the growth of the Teamsters across the Midwest and the rest of the country.

The story of the West Coast ports was largely the same, with union efforts again focused on stopping the movement of goods. After thousands of picketers were repelled by police, the union called a general strike. Like the other strikes of the time, the issue was whether the employer would be able to continue operations by hiring scabs. In the national textile strike, workers employed tactics such as sitting down on railroad tracks to stop the movement of finished goods.[14]

Spectacular as these strikes were, many progressives within the labor movement make a mistake in romanticizing them. While they rightly deserve our attention, these strikes must not obscure how mainstream stopping production—by any means necessary—was to the union movement of the 1930s. Conservative Teamster leaders like Jimmy Hoffa and Dave Beck believed in stopping production just as fervently as those on the left did. Likewise, even conservative leaders within the United Auto Workers (UAW) upheld the right to stop production. Homer Martin, the conservative first President of the United Auto Workers, stated that, "A strike can only be effective if and when it brings about a cessation of production. It is an absolute interference on the part of workers with the right of employers to make profit."[15] No matter their political stripes, stopping production was considered a mainstream union tactic in the 1930s.

THE SIT-DOWN STRIKE

One of the tactics most responsible for the growth of unions in the 1930s was the sit-down strike, which was, and continues to be, an excellent way for workers to stop production. The advantages of the sit-down strike are many: the employer cannot continue production since the workers occupy the plant; holding a plant is strategically easier than trying to defend dispersed picket lines; and having workers concentrated in one location helps maintain morale and unity among strikers.

According to Irving Bernstein, the sit-down strike was "to prove indispensable to the unionization" of the auto industry.[16] No better example of this exists than the 1936 rubber workers strike at Goodyear, Firestone, and Goodrich plants in Akron, Ohio. After getting jacked around by the company, the conservative American Federation of Labor (AFL) union, and the government for several years as they attempted to form a union, workers finally took matters into their own hands, sitting down over departmental disputes as a way of enforcing their demands. In early 1936, a series of plant wide strikes was followed by a mass strike of 18,000 workers.[17] The combination of sit-down strikes, combined with mass picketing and defiance of injunctions, helped gain union recognition for the rubber workers.

Perhaps the most well known use of the sit-down strike, and perhaps the most dramatic labor struggle of the 1930s, was by the United Autoworkers at General Motors in Flint, Michigan, the so-called "Flint Sit Down Strike." On December 30, 1936, autoworkers took over one of the General Motors plants upon learning that the company was planning to move machinery from it. On January 11, 1937, in what became known variously as the "Battle of Bulls Run" or the "Battle of the Running Bulls," Flint police attacked the picket lines and attempted to enter the plant. With union leader Victor Reuther (brother of future UAW president Walter Reuther) proclaiming that "everything hinges on the hinges," the strikers fired massive hinges down on the police, while supporters fought the police hand-to-hand in the streets.[18] After several more tense weeks, on February 11, 1937, GM settled with the UAW, giving the union bargaining rights in seventeen plants that had been shut down by the sit-down strike. Employees at the plants each received 5 percent raises, and more importantly, the UAW gained immediate legitimacy as a bargaining power for autoworkers.[19]

The General Motors sit-down strike contains several lessons for today's labor movement. First, the UAW knew that to win the strike, they needed to stop production. That is why they chose the sit-down tactic. Secondly, though the UAW represented a minority of autoworkers at GM at the time, union activists took the lead, banging on pipes to create a ruckus and to give their co-workers the strength to follow them, showing how a militant minority can make a difference. Third, the sit-down strike rested on a base of community and political support, as the workers understood that they needed to neutralize the government in order to prevent the deployment of troops to retake the plant. This required massive demonstrations of support from the surrounding community during the sit-down. Fourth, the strikers, the fledging UAW and even the leadership of the national Congress of Industrial Organizations (CIO) supported the strikers' right to occupy the plant.[20] Finally, the sit-down strikers knew they had to be willing to physically defend the plant. While they obviously could not win an all out battle with the National Guard, the fact that the Governor of Michigan, Frank Murphy, knew it would take a blood bath to get the strikers out of the plant was a deterrent to the use of force.

Following the success of the rubber workers in Akron and the UAW in Flint, use of the sit-down exploded across the nation. In 1937 alone, 400,000 workers participated in sit-down strikes, with employees as diverse as autoworkers, subway workers, factory workers, retail workers and garbage collectors all using the tactic.[21] According to Jeremy Brecher, author of *Strike*, the sit-down strike proved particularly useful for retail employees who could be easily replaced, such as Woolworth dime store workers in New York.

It is important to keep in mind that the sit-down strike wave of the 1930s occurred during a particular historical moment. Unions were on the march, and had a strong base within the working class. In addition, sentiment for an independent labor party ran high, and politicians in key industrial states could not ignore the demands of insurgent labor without risking provoking militant workers to desert the Democratic Party to form labor-based parties. This political leverage temporarily neutralized government power and limited the use of troops to retake struck plants. In this regard, the Flint sit-down strike shared many similarities with the 1934 Truckers strike in Minneapolis, where Minnesota's Farmer-Labor Party Governor Floyd Olson, like Michigan Governor Frank Murphy facing militant workers movements, hesitated to use government troops to bust the strike.

While this means we cannot simply import the tactics of the 1930s to today, we can still apply these historical examples—and particular, the emphasis that traditional trade unionists placed on stopping production—to the modern labor movement. An example of adapting traditional tactics to contemporary realities is the sit-down strike of workers at Republic Windows in 2008, which will be discussed later in this book.

Ultimately, the use of sit-down strike only lasted for a short period of time, and it was not long before the courts and the government reasserted control. After the brief and intense wave of strike activity, local authorities began to crack down and physically attack the worker occupations. "The sit-down's swift decline," wrote Rachel Mayer in *The Encyclopedia of Strikes*, "coincides with major changes in the extent of state repression, the legality of the tactic, and the nature of police intervention. In 1937, the conditions that made the sit-downs possible were rapidly changing as the political tide turned against the practice."[22]

LABOR'S HISTORICAL TOOLS OF SOLIDARITY

In conjunction with stopping production, the traditional labor movement stressed the building and maintaining of worker solidarity. Historically, the movement employed three different methods to attain solidarity: industry-wide strikes, secondary strikes, and secondary boycotts, all of which fall under the heading of "workplace-based solidarity." This is the most powerful form of solidarity, as it allows workers to band together to advance common interests.

INDUSTRY-WIDE STRIKES

Today, workers can legally strike only one employer at a time, and often at just one plant of that employer, which may be a large corporation with several plants throughout the country, or the world. Yet, until recent decades, striking an entire industry was a key tactic of the labor movement. At times, traditional strikes were massive national affairs, covering hundreds of thousands of workers. The great strikes in labor history—the Lawrence Bread and Roses textile strike or the great rail strikes—are still talked today about precisely because of their massive size. Unlike today's isolated workplace struggles, in these historic strikes, labor often joined together in confrontations involving tens or hundreds of thousands of workers.

Industry-wide strikes were important for many reasons. First, strikes encompassing multiple employers brought more workers into the struggle, which transformed what would otherwise have been an isolated action into a major battle between workers and employers. Thousands of workers striking at once also provided the sheer numbers required for massive rallies and for strikers to engage in confrontational activities. Large numbers of strikers also raised the profile of the conflict and made it easier to attract outside support.

In addition, many workers striking at once also helped to politicize the dispute, as politicians were forced to take sides in a clash between the working class and employers. The sheer scale of these strikes and their impact on the economy often prompted the government to intervene to prompt a settlement. Thus, the 1959 steel strike, which involved 500,000 workers and dragged on for 116 days, eventually required President Eisenhower to get involved in order to force a settlement. Industry-wide strikes also promoted a broad class-consciousness among employees, strengthening ties among both individual workers and the labor movement as a whole.

Certainly, not every strike of the first part of the twentieth century was industry-wide. Many were purely local battles, for instance, strikes pitting all of the miners against all of the mine operators in a particular region. Sometimes, workers would strike an individual employer who failed to adhere to union standards. Yet, even when a strike was not a large national affair, it was typically still part of an industry-wide strike approach.

SECONDARY STRIKES (AKA "SOLIDARITY STRIKES")

Another form of workplace-based solidarity is the secondary strike, or, as I like to call them, the solidarity strike. In a secondary strike, workers band together in solidarity with workers in other plants or even other industries. For example, let us assume that workers at a small auto parts manufacturer went on strike because their employer refused to pay industry standard wage rates. If the workers were able to enlist the support of Teamster drivers to refuse to transport parts, the United Auto Workers to refuse to build a car with the parts, and employees of car dealerships to refuse to sell the cars, the original strike against the auto parts manufacturer would be a primary strike and the others (the teamster drivers, the autoworkers, and the car dealership employees) would all be secondary strikes. By engaging in secondary strikes, workers are able act as a class and confront employers together, even though they have no immediate stake in the battle. That is workplace-based solidarity at its finest.

While union activists today often join other workers on the picket line or hold fundraisers for striking workers, secondary strikes represent solidarity of an entirely different order. With these workplace-based forms of solidarity, workers move beyond mere support for each other's struggles into directly confronting employers together. Solidarity strikes allow striking workers to put pressure on their company from several angles. While a regular (primary) strike, if successful, stops production at a given plant, a solidarity strike hits the employer at various points in the production and distribution chain. Thus, the union can choke off the supply chain to a struck employer or prevent the employer from distributing struck goods.

Solidarity strikes also leverage power by pressuring third party employers who may have relatively little interest in the dispute. Say, for example, that workers strike a brewery and set up picket lines at a popular bar in a working class neighborhood that sells beer from the struck brewery. In solidarity, the bar's workers decide to honor the picket line and go on strike as well. All of a sudden, a bar owner who has no direct financial interest in the matter is embroiled in a major labor conflict, and has no choice but to get rid of the scab-produced beer to separate her or his bar from the dispute.

During the strike at International Paper in the late 1980s, labor organizer Ray Rogers explained why the target was Coca Cola, rather than International Paper:

> International Paper is an $8 billion dollar company. If I take International Paper head on, I'm dealing with $8 billion worth of power, and they'll use all that power to destroy me....When I go after Coca Cola, on the other hand, I am not going after $8 billion worth of power, I'm only going after what the relationship between Coca Cola and International Paper is worth—maybe it's $25 million.[23]

This is why secondary tactics are so useful, as they allow unions to use corporate self-interest against other corporations. It leverages worker solidarity to destroy corporate solidarity.

In the 1930s and 1940s, Teamsters used solidarity tactics to expand their reach and organize the trucking industry as well as related industries, such as distribution centers, by refusing to handle goods at non-union firms. The employers would then either have to capitulate to Teamster demands or else see their goods spoil. Explains historian Donald Garnel:

> When an unorganized driver from the outlying area would pull into San Francisco or Oakland, his truck would be tied up without being unloaded. The employer was immediately contacted and notified that his truck would not be released and its freight unloaded until he went down to the head-quarters of the Teamster local in his area and signed the standard highway contract containing a union-shop clause.[24]

As with most other struggles of the 1930s, solidarity went hand in hand with stopping production. As Garnell notes, to organize the trucking industry, "The Teamsters threw up barriers to stop trucks to heading towards Oakland and San Francisco to check the membership status of drivers." [25] With intense employer opposition, thousands of small carriers, and innumerable owner operators, the Teamsters found that the "heavy hand proved to be far more effective than the kid glove."[26] Such tactics proved essential in transforming truck driving into an upper sector working class job.

Solidarity strikes, like industry-wide strikes, have benefits that far exceed their advantages in a given strike. For example, setting up picket lines at other employers was traditionally one way that strikes spread into larger confrontations. In the Pullman strike of 1894, the American Rail Union voted to boycott Pullman cars and conduct a solidarity strike. This turned a dispute between one manufacturer and its union into a major national strike. Many of the great strikes in labor history spread in this fashion.

LEVERAGING POWER: SECONDARY BOYCOTTS

The final major historical tactic to discuss is the secondary or solidarity boycott. For an example of this tactic, let us say that a group of workers strike their employer, Company A. The strikers would then ask fellow trade unionists and other workers to not only boycott products from Company A, but to also boycott any store that does business with Company A. So, if Store B sells Company A's products, the strikers would ask their fellow trade unionists as well as the public not to patronize Store B until it stopped selling the scab products. The boycott of the product from Company A is a primary boycott. The boycott of Store B is the solidarity (secondary) boycott.

Clearly, the solidarity boycott is far more effective than a regular consumer boycott, in which workers call for a boycott of a struck product. In that case, if workers strike a factory that produces tools, they have to convince millions of consumers not to buy the tools the company makes. Not surprisingly, that has rarely proven effective. But if workers target a store which sells the tools, they have only to convince one person—the owner of the store selling the struck product. Like with secondary strikes, the solidarity boycott drives a wedge between corporations, allowing unions to leverage their power.

In *Law and the Shaping of the American Labor Movement*, author William Forbath describes the use and power of citywide labor boycotts in the 1880s:

> If a city labor federation, for example, called a boycott against a brewer who persistently hired 'unfair' men or spurned union work rules, then it would do more than proclaim his beer 'unfair.' Representatives would visit saloons and call on them to cease serving his beer or face boycotts or picket lines themselves.[27]

Similarly, Phillip Foner discusses the frequent use of the boycott by the Knights of Labor in the mid-1880s:

> Boycotts were levied against newspapers, manufacturers and dealers in hats, cigars, clothing, carpets, dry goods, shoes, stoves, flour, beer, pianos and organs. Owners of hotels and theaters, and of excursion steamers, builders, coal-mining companies, and many others felt the pressure of the boycott. In practically every case, the boycott was also a secondary boycott, the person or firm disregarding the boycott being boycotted in turn.[28]

Forbath points out that unions eventually developed sophisticated national boycotts, where they would track the scab products, then go to other towns to enlist the support of the local labor movement to boycott the struck product and any business that sold it.

None of this is to say that the boycott was free of problems. Then, as now, they were difficult to sustain. As far back as 1885, one trade unionist complained that "to be a sincere and systematic boycotter now requires the carrying about of a catalogue of the different boycotted firms or articles; and, if you have a family, another catalogue is required for their use."[29] In 1913, Professor Henry Laidler of Columbia University described the difficulties of the boycott, saying that they were most effective for easily identifiable consumer goods, such as hats, whereas items like wood or iron were much more problematic.[30] Despite the problems, because they were so effective overall, courts, including the Supreme Court, eventually cracked down on solidarity boycotts.

OTHER TACTICS OF WAGE STANDARDIZATION

Traditional trade unions also employed several other tactics to accomplish wage standardization. Some of the earliest trade unions in the 1800s "legislated" labor standards, where the unions would agree internally on a fair wage rate or work rules and then demand that the employer adopt these standards. Employers who failed to meet the standards were branded as "unfair" and subject to a strike or boycott. At the same time, workers who violated the standards were declared to be scabs, since the wages were the concern of all workers in the industry and it was believed that one group of workers did not have the right to undercut the wages of others.

A related tactic, outlawed as part of the Taft-Hartley Act in 1947, was the closed shop. The closed shop required employers to hire only union workers, giving unions control over the supply of labor. Employers understood the importance of these tactics, and organized to break the union monopoly on labor. As related in William Milliken's fascinating history, *A Union Against Unions*, unions in the Twin Cities opposed publicly funded trade schools organized through the Citizens Alliance, arguing "we know, by indisputable evidence, that wherever such schools have been established, either under private or public control, they are breeders for strikebreakers."[31]

THE LESSONS OF THE 1930S FOR TODAY'S LABOR MOVEMENT

The 1930s showed, most dramatically, that the basis of union power was an assertion of control over the workplace in order to halt production until worker demands were met. As described in the labor relations textbook *The Practice of Collective Bargaining*, a strike "denies the employer the use of a productive plant until it is ransomed by a satisfactory settlement."[32] In basic industries during the 1930s, the backbone of resistance to industrial unionism was broken by the heroic actions of trade unionists resisting employers, courts and even the government.

In many ways, the tactics of the 1930s were developed to fight against exactly the same problems facing trade unions today, namely an employer determined to continue production, with no shortage of scabs to take strikers' jobs. If one believes that the unions of the 1930s were justified in stopping production, then there is no basis to say that today's labor movement is not equally justified in utilizing similar tactics.

The other great lesson of the 1930s was the power of solidarity. For example, the 1934 truckers strike in the Twin Cities involved all truck drivers in the city striking at once, encompassing dozens of employers. In contrast, how would the same strike have played out under today's system of labor control? First off, the Teamsters would probably hold elections with each trucking company, perhaps contending with arguments that truckers were independent contractors. Even if the union actually won all of these individual organizing campaigns, which is a big assumption, they would have to then bargain separately with each trucking company. Assuming the workers were brave enough to strike at a given company, the union would have to put up picket lines at the individual companies and then most likely watch scabs stream in to take their union jobs. Needless to say, if the Teamsters of the 1930s had used today's tactics, they would have lost the battle to unionize the industry. Fortunately, to the great benefit of generations of truck drivers and their families, the Twin Cities Teamsters of 1934 played by labor's rules, not management's.

One can go industry-by-industry and see how the trade unionists of the 1930s developed effective tactics for stopping production. It is also important to realize that these tactics were not confined to left-wing unionists. Sometimes, by focusing on the major battles such as the 1934 Teamsters strike, the giant confrontations in rail in the 1800s, or the important battles led by the Industrial Workers of the World (IWW), labor activists lose sight of how important stopping production was to even moderate or conservative trade unionists of the past.

While the contemporary labor movement flounders for strategies to move forward, it ignores the clear answers from history, at its own peril. Today, management has constructed a system of labor control that has contorted the strike, once an instrument of human freedom and dignity, into a free market perversion. The contemporary labor movement needs a strike based on labor' economics, not those of management, based on labor's values, not management's. Like the trade unionists of the 1930s, today's labor movement must prioritize developing effective strike tactics which hold the promise of improving workers' lives.

To be clear, unionists cannot simply import traditional union tactics into today's world, as much has changed since the 1930s: workers are no longer concentrated in dense urban centers, the labor left in this country is weak, and unionists face a transformed economy dominated by massive global corporations. However, trade unionists have always had to adapt to constantly changing conditions and shifting employer strategies. The main problem is not that trade unionists have been unable to overcome these obstacles and create an effective strike in the past. The problem is that today, they are not even trying.

3. THE OUTLAWING OF SOLIDARITY AND THE DECLINE OF THE STRIKE

These days, worker solidarity, for decades the heart and soul of trade unionism, has, for the most part, been outlawed. This did not occur overnight, but was the result of a complicated, decades-long legislative and legal assault by employers against the foundations of unionism. The outlawing of solidarity began with the passage of the National Labor Relations Act (NLRA) in 1935, became explicit with the passage of the Taft-Hartley Act of 1947, and was furthered along by Supreme Court decisions in the 1960s.

The National Labor Relations Act, commonly referred to as the Wagner Act after its sponsor, Senator Robert F. Wagner, is the foundation of modern labor relations. The Act provides a comprehensive set of regulations of covering most private sector workers in the United States, with the exception of rail and airline employers—who are covered under the Railway Labor Act—government employees, and some private sector employees such as farm workers and employees of small firms. The NLRA governs the legal formation of unions, details the obligation to collectively bargain, and makes certain union and employer conduct illegal.

The fundamental problem with the NLRA is in its underlying philosophy, which treats the decision to unionize as a choice involving only the employees of an individual employer. In contrast, trade unionism prior to the NLRA was geared towards establishing common standards in an industry. Even before its passage, many trade unionists of the 1930s were aware of the NLRA's potential danger to the labor movement. According to author and legal scholar Christopher Tomlins, AFL craft unions worried that passage of the NLRA would

> ...result in the creation of a weak and atomized labor movement consisting of thousands of uncoordinated groups. [AFL President] William Green voiced that concern in 1934: 'elections in individual plants supported by the National Labor Board should not be confused with real collective bargaining....In the long run we must look to independent organizations of workers on a national or international basis for real collective bargaining.[1]

Traditional trade unionists believed that the choice to unionize should not be left not to individual workers, but to the union as a whole, which they viewed as the agent responsible for setting standards for workers in a given industry. The logic behind this reasoning was that, if the decision to unionize was left to employees at individual shops, the workers at one shop could choose to remain non-union, which could then undercut union workers throughout an entire industry. This in turn would undermine the very purpose of trade unions, which is to standardize wages in a labor market. This difference, between the economic necessity to standardize wages and the underlying philosophy of the NLRA, presents a major difficulty for the revival of trade unions.

Under the framework established by the NLRA, contemporary unionism is based upon elections at individual employers, followed by collective bargaining with those individual employers. Gone is the historical role of the union as the protector of minimum standards, and what is left in its wake is a legal definition of the union as the agent of workers, just like an insurance agent or a lawyer. By transforming the question of unionism into one of representation elections, the NLRA opened the door for employers and the government to interject themselves into workers' decisions to form a union. As labor historian David Brody argues, "the representation election is the instrument by which labor's enemies have hijacked the law."[2]

Despite the stranglehold that the NLRA placed on unions, they were still able to prosper from through the 1960s, as the solidarity and militancy displayed by the labor movement in the 1930s did not die out easily. Unions of the period avoided the NLRA's restrictions by banding together across employers in multi-employer agreements, at times covering hundreds of thousands of workers in industries such as steel and mining. In other industries such as auto, the United Auto Workers (UAW) would bargain with one employer and then apply the pattern established there to the rest of the industry. This is what is known as "pattern bargaining." However, over the years, employers relentlessly attacked such uses of solidarity, through both legislation and legal means.

THE "SLAVE LABOR ACT"

Following a decade of worker advancement, employers in the 1940s began a counteroffensive against the labor movement, targeting, in particular, the tactics of workplace-based solidarity. This campaign to eliminate solidarity set the stage for one of the sharpest legislative battles in U.S. labor history: the fight over the Taft-Hartley amendments to the NLRA in 1947. Soon after the NLRA was upheld as constitutional by the Supreme Court, a surprised business community began to organize to undermine the Act. The Chamber of Commerce and the National Association of Manufacturers in particular began "a long range program to influence public opinion" against the NLRA.[3] They proposed amendments, bought news papers ads and advanced arguments that the NLRA had tilted the playing field against employers. Between 1937 and the passage of Taft-Hartley in 1947, 230 bills were introduced in Congress (along with numerous others in state legislatures), all to curb union power.

Following the end of World War II, the Republican Party launched a counter-offensive against FDR's New Deal programs, with a special emphasis placed on reversing the gains of the labor movement. Rather than repeal the NLRA entirely, business sought to amend it in such a way as to hamstring unions. Following huge gains in the 1946 mid-term elections, Republicans launched a major effort to gut the NLRA. Despite the labor movement's heroic efforts to stop it, the Taft-Hartley Act passed Congress by overwhelming margins, with even a majority of Democrats in both the House and Senate supporting it. Congress then voted to override President Truman's veto, and Taft-Hartley became law.

During the battle, trade unionists had denounced Taft-Hartley as the "Slave Labor Act," believing that its passage would lead to the destruction of the labor movement. Unfortunately, they were correct. Historian Nelson Lichtenstein writes about how union leaders of the 1940s understood the potentially apocalyptic effect of Taft-Hartley. Congress of Industrial Organizations (CIO) President Phillip Murray stated that, "if that bill becomes law, in the course of time under its operation ... the trends are and the powers have so decreed, that we should have a type of Fascist, capitalistic control over the lives of men, women, and children."[4] AFL leader George Meany opposed the legislation because "the Taft-Hartley Act's restrictions upon trade union use of the boycott, as well as its more general efforts to limit the spread of unionization, made more difficult the equalization of wages and conditions among competing firms within the same industry." According to Lichtenstein, Meany believed that Taft-Hartley would pit "worker against worker in a downward spiral that [would transform] human labor into a mere commodity and workers into chattels."[5]

On the other side, the rhetoric of employers was equally inflammatory, as they viewed passage of Taft-Hartley as necessary to prevent "totalitarian" labor control of the economy. Notes Lichtenstein: "The half-century old rhetoric still blisters with a passion that cannot be ignored: slavery, servitude, freedom, liberty, and redemption were words both opponents and supporters of the Taft-Hartley Act hurled at each other."[6] The heated rhetoric between the two sides demonstrates the watershed quality of Taft-Hartley, which ended up being extremely beneficial to employers, while devastating unions. Among the anti-union provisions in Taft-Hartley were the banning of the closed shop, the permitting of states to establish "right to work" (right to scab) laws, and attacks against the "Communist" leadership of trade unions.

However, arguably the most significant anti-union feature of Taft-Hartley was its effect on workplace-based solidarity. The Act not only banned solidarity strikes and boycotts, but also required the National Labor Relations Board to go to court to seek injunctions against unions that utilized these tactics. This was no accident, as employers and their representatives in Congress understood that to break the rising union movement they needed to destroy worker solidarity. Thus, Taft-Hartley legally prevented workers from banding together and supporting each other's picket lines in a meaningful way, in the procress outlawing citywide shutdowns and the use of solidarity strikes and boycotts. In one fell swoop, Taft-Hartley made illegal the very tactics most responsible for labor's successes in the 1930s.

In the late 1950's, Congress further tightened the noose against unions, passing the Landrum Griffin Act in 1959, which prohibited "hot cargo" agreements. During the 1950s, workers at unionized employers would negotiate what were known as hot cargo clauses, which stated that they did not have to handle any goods produced by a struck or non-union shop. Landrum Griffin made such clauses illegal, preventing unions from negotiating over a topic of vital concern to their membership—the right to refuse to handle scab goods.

Many of the problems unions face today can be traced back to the passage of the Taft-Hartley Act. One reason that labor has been unable to stop the growth of the non-union sector in retail, for example, is its inability to use solidarity to choke off the supply lines of the budding Wal-Marts and Target superstores. Taft-Hartley also restricts the right of workers to set up picket lines at a worksite other than their own, and to leaflet workers of another employer in order to get them to strike.

These limitations on picketing and secondary activity violate the freedom of speech and the right to association established in the First Amendment of the U.S. Constitution. Yet, under Taft-Hartley, workers are afforded considerably less protection under the law than other protesters. To illustrate this second-class treatment of workers, law professor James Pope uses the example of three picketers standing outside a toy store.[7] One is a trade unionist with a picket sign urging a boycott of the store for selling toys made by a struck shop. The second is someone urging customers to buy toys at the store. The third person is a student anti-sweatshop activist picketing the unfair treatment of Asian workers who made the toys that are sold in the store. In this scenario, only the trade unionist would be denied constitutional protection and be subject to arrest and fines.

Given that the labor movement viewed the rules outlawing solidarity to be of such vital importance back in the 1930s and 1940s, one would assume that freeing itself of these restrictions would be at the center of any discussion about the movement's current predicament. After all, history has clearly shown the detrimental effect of Taft-Hartley on unions. However, the numerous books on labor written in the last decade, from mainstream officials like John Sweeney and Andy Stern to those on the left, have all ignored the outlawing of solidarity's central role in the labor movement's decline. At this point, only advocates of the Labor Party and, outside the labor movement, Ralph Nader, consistently raise the issue of trying to get rid of Taft-Hartley restrictions.

In reality, once labor began allowing the government the ability to restrict trade union activity, the slippery slope from the strong labor movement of the 1930s to today's feeble strike had begun. As a matter of fact, many of the restrictions in Taft-Hartley were already being implemented in the early 1940s by the labor board and the courts, before the Act had even become law. Legal historian Christopher Tomlins notes that "the Taft-Hartley Act thus proved much less of a break with the past than has been usually assumed."[8] The passage of the Act just sped up the process. As the American Civil Liberties Union argued at the time of the NLRA's passage in 1935, "the pressures on any governmental agency from employers are so constant and determined that it is far better to have no government intervention than to suffer the delusion that it will aid labor in its struggle for the rights to organize, bargain collectively, and strike." [9]

THE GUTTING OF INDUSTRY-WIDE BARGAINING

Another goal of the anti-solidarity forces was the elimination of industry-wide bargaining. According to Nelson Lichtenstein, when Taft-Hartley passed in 1947, some sections of capital sought a provision prohibiting industry-wide bargaining, "because they saw it leading inexorably to the kind of class solidarity, politicized bargaining, and governmental intervention from which they were trying to escape."[10] For example, the head of the National Association of Manufacturers, "… attacked industry-wide bargaining primarily because he recognized that only when an entire industry was shut down did the unions have the leverage to bring the state in on their side."[11]

Even though restrictions on multi-employer bargaining were expressly rejected by Congress when it passed the Taft-Hartley Act, employers kept up a steady drumbeat of pressure against industry-wide bargaining throughout the 1950s, arguing that it gave unions a monopoly. Eventually, this pressure paid off, as during the 1960s, a series of court decisions held that multi-employer bargaining required the agreement of both the union and the company.[12] Therefore, by simply notifying a union prior to the commencement of negotiations, a company could free itself of multi-employer bargaining requirements. In effect, industry-wide bargaining became a completely voluntary—and one-sided—arrangement, as a union insisting on negotiating on an industry-wide basis in the face of employer opposition could be found in violation in the NLRA.[13]

Notwithstanding these legal changes, industry-wide bargaining remained important well into the 1970s, as employers did not generally challenge union power, preferring instead to chip away at the edges. Many employers, in fact, preferred the stability of multi-employer bargaining and did not attempt break free from industry-wide patterns. It was not until the 1980s that employers fully utilized their hard-won legal tools to try to eliminate industry-wide bargaining. Indeed, a large part of the employer offensive of the 1980s consisted of employers attacking industry-wide bargaining and pattern agreements with a vengeance. In industries such as meatpacking, steel and trucking, patterns covering hundreds of thousands of workers collapsed into a race to the bottom,[14] as "companies demanded that local unions make concessions, usually on working conditions or work rules, with the threat that if they didn't give in the work would go elsewhere."[15] Whereas previously unions had understood that "standard wages, benefits and conditions [were] the economic foundations of unionism," in the new paradigm, even unions in the same company were forced to compete against one another for work.[16] Even when local unions attempted to fight back, they were often undercut by other locals within the same company. While in the 1930s, unions had been built through solidarity, by the 1980s, they were being destroyed by a lack of solidarity.

NO STRIKE CLAUSES AND SOLIDARITY

The decline in solidarity cannot be blamed completely on the government, employers, and the courts, however, as in the decades following labor's advances in the 1930s, labor officials willingly gave up the right to engage in solidarity by allowing the inclusion of no-strike clauses in union contracts. While few union contracts in the 1930s contained no-strike clauses, many labor leaders nevertheless disapproved of relying on shop floor power, which often took the form of plant walkouts and slowdowns.[17] These same officials took steps to reassert control following the turmoil of the 1930s, agreeing to no-strike clauses and working to curb grassroots militancy. Labor activist Staughton Lynd notes that labor "radicalism did not die a natural death in the CIO unions but was brutally purged."[18]

Unlike the restrictions on solidarity contained in Taft-Hartley, which were imposed on the labor movement despite vigorous opposition, no-strike clauses were primary self-inflicted wounds because many unions freely allowed the incorporation of these clauses in their contracts. Essentially, unions gave up their right to engage in workplace-based solidarity. As a result, during the years following World War II, more and more union contracts came to include no-strike clauses. While the breadth of these clauses varied, they were often used as a justification to allow one union to continue to work while other employees at the same plant or employer were on strike.

There has always been a tension within trade unionism between the need for workers to act as a class to fight the power of corporations and the limited scope of bargaining. Therefore, the issue of no-strike clauses and honoring of contracts has caused difficulties since the earliest days of trade unions. The problem is simple. Unions reach agreements with employers in the form of a contract, which both sides agrees to honor. However, when workers strike during the term of the agreement, employers question why they should try to reach a labor agreement if unions are going to strike. In the view of management, by striking, workers are not honoring their contract. At the same time, workers need to act as a class in order to make gains. If some workers are locked into a contract that forbids them from striking, solidarity is undercut.

Thus, responding to management pressure, no strike provisions were strongly pushed by the Supreme Court in its quest to outlaw worker solidarity. In the late 1930s, in *NLRB vs. Sands Manufacturing Co.*, the Court ruled that the company had not violated the NLRA by discharging workers who struck during the term of their contract in order to have the provisions of the agreement changed.[19] Forty years later, in a series of cases in the 1970s, the Supreme Court issued injunctions forbidding workers to strike during the term of their contract.[20]

In doing so, the Court ignored the explicit provisions of the 1932 Norris LaGuardia Act, which was passed to prevent judges from intervening in labor disputes. The Act states in clear terms that Federal Courts have no jurisdiction to issue injunctions except in very limited circumstances.[21] Throughout the 1930s and 1940s, the Norris LaGuardia Act had worked as intended, with courts largely refraining from intervening in labor disputes. However, this was to be short lived, as employers attacked the federal policy against injunctions through Congress via the Taft

Hartley Act, as well as through the courts.

The Taft Hartley Act undermined the protection against the injunctions in two ways.[22] First, it mandated that the National Labor Relations Board seek injunctions when it determined that unions were violating secondary strike and boycott provisions. Taft Hartley also allowed the President of the United States to intervene in labor disputes and obtain emergency injunctions in cases that allegedly imperiled the national health and safety. These two provisions undermined the LaGuardia Act, which had been one of labor's main congressional victories of the 1930s.

The Supreme Court further took back the power that Congress had expressly taken from it when decided in *Boys Market v Retail Clerks Local 770* (1970) that despite the clear language of the Norris LaGuardia Act, federal courts could enjoin strikes which violated a contractual no strike clause. The Court based its decision on the supposed federal preference for arbitration over strikes. A mere four years after the case, the Supreme Court broadened its ruling, holding that even where the parties had not agreed to a no strike clause, a strike could be enjoined because it contained an arbitration clause.[23]

Despite these rulings, nowhere in the Norris LaGuardia Act is there any evidence that Congress intended to allow the judiciary to issue injunctions in these instances. Congress was unambiguous: Federal Courts did not have any jurisdiction to issue injunctions in labor disputes except as provided in the Norris LaGuardia Act. Notably, the *Boys Market* decision was written by liberal Justice William Brennan, reflecting how, as with many other Supreme Court decisions limiting solidarity, it was often liberal judges leading the charge.[24]

RESTRICTING PICKET-LINE MILITANCY

To further reign in union power, employers also understood that picket line militancy needed to be eliminated. No case better illustrates this than the Fansteel decision. In February 1937, one hundred workers at the Fansteel Metallurgical Corporation in Waukeegan, Illinois resorted to a sit-down strike after the company refused to follow the law and recognize the union that the workers were trying to form. Despite the illegality of the employer's action, "On the advice of Fansteel's attorney, they [the police] rigged a two-story assault tower mounted on a ten-ton truck. Arriving before sunrise, the police found the sixty defenders asleep. Officers positioned in the assault tower blasted tear-gas canisters through the factory windows at point-blank range."[25] Ultimately, the sit-down strikers were fired.

The workers sued, and two years later, in 1939, the case reached The Supreme Court. In *NLRB vs. Fansteel Metallurgical Corporation*, the Court ruled that the sit-down strike was unprotected by the NLRA, and that the company did not violate the law by firing the workers.[26] As a result of this decision, Fansteel was able to bust the legitimate union and form a company union in its place, which had, as the final decision maker in the grievance procedure, the company president. Legal scholar James Pope points out the double standard of the Supreme Court in the Fansteel case:

> Why was it legal for Fansteel to terminate employees for responding with self-help to its own statutory violations? The opinion made it clear that the employer's common-law property rights were of a different and higher order than the employees' statutory labor rights. While the company's repeated violations of the workers' right to organize did not deprive the company of "its legal rights to the possession and protection of its property," the workers' violation of the employer's property rights put them "outside the protection of the statute."[27]

In the years following the Fansteel decision, the courts and the NLRB found a wide range of picket line activity to be unprotected under the NLRA.[28] In addition to sit-down strikes, actions such as mass picketing and certain types of verbal statements against scabs were found to be impermissible strike activity, which meant that workers could be lawfully fired and unions fined or otherwise punished for engaging in these activities.

The 1954 strike of the Kohler factory in Wisconsin demonstrates how, in less than twenty years, picket line militancy had essentially been quashed.[29] Back in 1934, employees of the Kohler Company had tried to organize a union over the objections of the company president, Walter J. Kohler. Kohler was virulently antiunion, and believed that while workers could organize, unions should not have exclusive bargaining power, as claimed by the newly formed AFL Union of Kohler workers. After Kohler refused to negotiate, the workers declared a strike, which turned violent when "special deputies broke through the picket lines to escort a coal car that strikers had turned back. A battle ensued outside the plant that left two strikers dead and over 40 wounded. The next day, Governor Schmedeman called out the National Guard to restore order."[30]

Twenty years later, in April of 1954, the longest major labor dispute in U.S. history began when UAW workers at Kohler stormed out in a disagreement over demands for higher wages and fringe benefits. For the first fifty days of the strike, the UAW employed mass picketing, with at times thousands of workers blockading the plant. Then after much legal wrangling, in a case that eventually reached the United States Supreme Court, the Wisconsin Employment Relations Board issued an injunction against the picketers.[31] Unlike in the 1930s, the union complied with the injunction, allowing the plant to resume production with nonunion labor, setting off six years of intermittent violence. Finally, in 1960 the NLRB ruled that Kohler had refused to bargain in good faith after the strike began, and ordered it to reinstate the workers who were still on strike. Despite this ruling, it would still take an additional two years before the company and the union could agree on a contract.[32]

The Kohler strike reveals how much picket line militancy had declined in two decades. At the start of the strike, the UAW understood that it needed to stop production. However, after only two months, complying with a court injunction, the union stopped mass picketing, which allowed production to continue. By bringing the strike into the courts, Kohler was able to have the dispute judged on a more favorable terrain, as by the mid-1950s, the legal system essentially prohibited effective picket line activities, which allowed Kohler to fire the workers who engaged in the plant blockades. Most importantly, Kohler was able to change the narrative. Whereas in the 1930s, union members upheld the right to an effective picket line and derided those who attempted to break it up, by the 1950s, strikers using the very same tactics were treated as criminals. Thus, Kohler was able to reframe the issue as one of union violence, as opposed to the 1930s, when unions were generally portrayed as the victims of employer attacks on peaceful picket lines. Over the next quarter century, this pro-management narrative would come to prevail, at the expense of workers.

PERMANENT REPLACEMENT OF STRIKING WORKERS

To many trade unionists, President Reagan's 1981 firing of the striking air traffic controllers represented by the Professional Air Traffic Controllers Organization (PATCO) was a crucial event, signaling the federal government's endorsement of open warfare on workers. While Reagan's actions are certainly noteworthy when discussing the decline of the labor movement, in truth, the permanent replacement of striking workers had been going on long before the firing of the air traffic controllers. A 2008 study concluded that, "the increasing use of permanent replacements predates the events of the infamous Professional Air Traffic Controllers Organization (PATCO) strike. By the mid-1970s, unions were increasingly concerned about the use of permanent replacements as an offensive weapon by hostile employers."[33]

The seeds of permanent replacements actually goes back to 1939, when the Supreme Court, in one of the first court cases interpreting the National Labor Relations Act, ruled in *NLRB vs. Mackay Radio and Telegraph Co.* that an employer could "permanently replace" striking workers. This ruling came to be known as the "Mackay Doctrine" and has become one of the most significant factors in the weakening of the modern labor movement. Under the Mackay Doctrine, employers can hire scabs during a strike and, at the conclusion of the strike, keep the scabs as regular employees, though they must allow striking workers to return as vacancies occur. While the striker is not technically dismissed, and can conceivably get his or her job back eventually, this distinction meant little when workers are out of work and cannot pay their bills. This scenario played out countless times in the 1980s and 1990s, where workers went out on strike, the company hired "permanent" scabs, the strike ended, yet the scabs kept working at the expense of the strikers.

The *Mackay Radio* decision, which has become enshrined in labor law, goes directly against the wording of the National Labor Relations Act (NLRA), which states that

> Employees shall have the right to self- organization, to form, join, or assist labor organizations, to bargain collectively through representatives of their own choosing, and to engage in other concerted activities for the purpose of collective bargaining or other mutual aid or protection.

The NLRA further provides that it is a violation "to interfere with, restrain, or coerce" employees in the exercise of these rights.

The NLRA is very clear—a strike is supposed to be a legally protected form of activity. However, laws are just words on paper, and courts can, and will, interpret them in any way they choose. And, over the past seventy years, the legal system in this country has consistently interpreted labor law with a pro-management bias. In a 1990 law review article, Mathew Finken showed how, following up on the *Mackay Radio* decision, successive Supreme Court rulings closed off tactics that unions could use against scabs. The end result is that

> In the face of an impending strike, the employer may announce a decision to permanently to replace strikers, to offer advantageous treatment to cross-overs, and to give preference to replacements and cross-overs over un-reinstated strikers in any recall after a later lay-off. After the strike is commenced, the employer may issue an ultimatum to return to work or face permanent replacement; indeed, such is a recommended practice.[34]

Finken concluded that the "statutory 'right' to strike" has turned out for many workers to be "an exercise in permanent job loss, and, for the union, an act of potential self-immolation."[35] Faced with such a stacked legal deck, many contemporary trade unionists have either stopped striking completely, or adopted less effective second cousins of the strike, such as the one-day publicity strike.

Despite the 1939 Mackay ruling that strikers could be permanently replaced, for the three decades that followed, the tactic was used sparingly by management, largely because of the strength of the labor movement of the time, which would not accept the employer's right to continue operating with scabs. Instead, most employers ceased production during a strike; those who did not made due with supervisors and temporary scabs, until the strike had run its course and the regular workers returned. Albert Rees, writing in 1962, stated that,

> Until about 1940, it was common for employers to attempt to operate struck plants, using non-striking employees or new employees recruited for the purpose. Unions engaged in mass picketing to prevent the strikebreakers or "scabs" from entering the plant....Since World War II it has been unusual for employer to attempt to operate during a strike.[36]

Thus, the Mackay Doctrine initially had a negligible impact, as strikers used tactics such as the picket line to block scabs from entering struck plants. In addition, large industrial unions used mass demonstrations and political pressure to keep law enforcement from getting involved in labor disputes. While employers were officially allowed to continue operations during a strike, "an unofficial norm barred them from doing so."[37] This "unofficial norm" was confirmed by labor economist Neil Chamberlain, who wrote in the mid-1960s that, "Commonly now when union and management negotiators face the reality of a strike, they proceed to call out the workers and then close the plants with businesslike regard for plant, equipment, and future production."[38]

While there are no hard statistics on the use of the historical use of permanent replacements, by analyzing NLRB cases and the statements of practitioners, Michael H. LeRoy of the University of Illinois has determined that the use of permanent replacements was uncommon in the 1950s, ticked up in the 1960s and 1970s, and became widespread in the 1980s as a renewed aggressiveness on the part of management dovetailed with a breakdown of solidarity among trade union leaders.[39] On a related note, labor scholar Joseph McCartin studied the use of permanent replacement scabs in the 1970s and found that the "normalization of the tactic in the public sector paved the way for its expanded use in the private sector."[40]

Once the floodgates were opened, permanently replacing workers became the employer weapon of choice during labor disputes, with predictably disastrous results for workers. According to the Bureau of National Affairs, "More than 55,000 striking workers saw permanent replacements fill their jobs in 1990 and 1991…and 55 percent or approximately 29,000 did not return to their jobs at the conclusion of the dispute."[41] Using the threat of permanent replacement, employers also became increasingly aggressive in collective bargaining. The General Accounting Office found that

> seven out of eight union representatives and two out of three employer representatives believed that permanent replacements were used "more often" or "far more often" in the late 1980s than the late 1970s. In 1985 and 1989, one-quarter of employers said they would use permanent replacements and fifteen percent had actually used permanent replacements in economic strikes.[42]

Since permanent replacements had been rarely utilized in strikes prior to the 1980s, when management began to embrace the tactic, there were, unsurprisingly, spontaneous outbursts by strikers. For example, the Greyhound strike of 1983 saw hundreds of strikers arrested in protest. Similarly, in construction, when nonunion firms first broke into a local construction market, workers often responded aggressively. While the issue was usually posed by management as one of picket line violence by the strikers, the actions of the workers were in fact rational economic responses to scabs taking their jobs. Historically, unions had always taken the position that they were defending the picket line against attempts by management to replace the strikers with scabs. Thus, any violence that occurred was employer-created. As labor commentator Jack Barbash explained in the 1950s, "When the employer thinks that he can break the strike by operating the plant and getting the employees to go through the picket line, violence in greater or lesser degree is likely to occur."[43] By the 1980s, the victims of employer aggression—the workers—were now being characterized as inciting violent, merely for defending their picket lines, and their jobs. As a result, unions started spending a considerable amount of effort to get picketers to fall in line, in order to avoid injunctions. This created a very different climate from the 1930s, when trade unions, rather than suppressing worker outrage, employed militancy to stop production and win strikes.

THE EMPLOYER OFFENSIVE OF THE 1980S

The system of collective bargaining that was in place from the 1940s through the 1970s, although appearing to favor labor, actually masked increasing union weakness. Internally, unions grew more bureaucratic and staff driven. Bargaining became something done by "experts" behind closed doors. At the same time, Congress and the Supreme Court were undermining the very basis of stable collective bargaining. Perhaps the most significant problem for unions during this time, however, was that they abandoned the very tactics that had produced their power in the first place. Labor forgot that the point of a picket line was to prevent scabs from taking strikers' jobs, and stopped engaging in industry-wide solidarity. Without these traditional tactics, unions were defenseless against the employer onslaught of the 1980s.

Corresponding to the decline of the U.S. economy in the 1970s, employers intensified their resistance to collective bargaining. Following the concessions by workers at Chrysler in 1979, employers began demanding—and gaining—concessions in a variety of industries, from airlines to meatpacking to steel.[44] Employers won decreases in wages and benefits and the elimination of cost of living clauses, as well as two-tier wage scales, and the gutting of work rules. The most glaring sign of labor's concessionary stance was that the average collectively bargained wage rate in 1986 was a negative amount. It was the era of union concessions.

To some on the left of the labor movement, the main problem during this time was that unions did not fight back against employer aggressiveness. Certainly, it is true that many top leaders of international unions, accustomed to years of accommodation with management, were reluctant to attack employers, instead agreeing to concessions to try to staunch the tide. This strategy did not work, as corporations saw blood in the water and began demanding more and more givebacks from workers.

Even when unions did take a stand, they usually lost, the main reason being that, unlike in the 1930s, the unions of the 1980s failed to stop production. Nor did workers band together across workplaces or industries to fight employers. In a typical strike of the 1980s, workers at one plant or employer struck. Then, after a short period of time, the employer would bring in scabs. With production continuing, employers were able to win strike after strike. While unions could have fought harder in the 1980s, the problem was not mainly a question of willpower; it was a question of tactics. In fact, during this time, unions engaged in more bitter struggles than today's allegedly more progressive unions do.

The 1983 Arizona Copper Mine strike is representative of the period. Mineworkers at the Phelps Dodge copper mill in Morenci, Arizona were members of the United Steelworkers of America. Phelps Dodge came into the negotiations spoiling for a fight, convinced that they could beat the union by employing new, aggressive bargaining tactics. Announcing its demands in the media prior to the start of negotiations, the company asked for wage cuts, concessions on health care and vacation, and the end to cost of living adjustments. They also demanded the elimination of all side letters governing work rules and changes to workers' schedules. The union—which would have had to break the pattern agreement in the industry in order to accept the company's proposals—went on strike in July of 1983.*

A little over a month into the strike, Phelps Dodge began to hire permanent replacement workers. In protest, two thousand mineworkers stormed the company's employment office. The next day, after rejecting a ten-day moratorium, workers threatened to storm the mine, which would have forced the company to shut down production. At this point, under pressure from Phelps Dodge, Democratic Governor Bruce Babbitt called out the National Guard to escort scabs and bust the strike. Once the National Guard intervened, it was just a matter of time before the strike was lost.

The failure of the Phelps Dodge strike was not surprising, as the workers lacked the tactics necessary for victory. For example, aside from the spontaneous outbursts of picketers, the union did not systematically attempt to stop production. With the union making no attempt to block access to the plant, their only "strategy"—if one can call it that—was to set up picket lines and hope that the scabs would not cross. But, as trade unionists discovered time and time again during the 1980s, employers had no problem finding scabs to take striking workers' jobs. Too add insult to injury, once the strike was defeated, the scabs at Phelps Dodge voted out the union. Phelps Dodge had not only won the strike, they had also destroyed the union in the process.

---

*The strike is well documented by Jonathan Rosenblum in *Copper Crucible: How the Arizona Miners' Strike of 1983 Recast Labor-Management Relations in America*, as well as by noted author Barbara Kingsolver's *Holding the Line: Women in the Great Arizona Mine Strike of 1983.*

According to author Jonathan Rosenblum, the "Phelps Dodge strike is emblematic of the decline of two vital achievements of the American labor movement: solidarity and the right to strike."[45] The Phelps Dodge strikers fought their battle virtually alone. And, unlike unions of the past, they fought with their hands tied behind their backs. Whereas trade unionists of the 1930s and 1940s understood that to win a strike the union must physically stop production, the union at Phelps Dodge had no such strategy to win the strike.

Soon, the script established in Arizona became commonplace across the nation. Pick an industry in the 1980s and 1990s, and you can easily find a strike where workers were permanently replaced. In the airline industry, flight attendants at TWA discovered that they were replaceable when the carrier hired scabs to take their jobs in 1986. In transit, Greyhound workers struck in 1990, with the employer hiring permanent replacement scabs. Throughout the 1980s and 1990s, skilled workers such as air traffic controllers, mechanics, and pilots all incorrectly assumed that they could not be replaced by scabs.

In certain instances, such as at Phelps Dodge and International Paper at Jay, Maine in the early 1990s, the union was de-certified following the end of the strike. After one year of an economic strike, workers who have not been recalled are no longer eligible to vote in union elections.[46] Therefore, an employer who wanted to get rid of a union could provoke a strike, hire scabs, wait a year, then have the scabs vote out the union. Not only would the company win the strike, but the plant would also become non-union. The strike thus became a weapon for the employer to rid themselves of unions for good.

Following the defeat and permanent replacement of striking paper workers at the International Paper plant in Jay, Maine, the issue of banning permanent replacement scabs became a major political initiative of the AFL-CIO. A bill barring the use of permanent replacement scabs passed the House of Representatives in 1992 and 1994 but fell to Republican filibusters both times, with Democratic senators from the south failing to support both bills. However, by the mid-1990s, the issue of permanent replacement scabs almost completely disappeared from labor's radar. After the failed attempts to amend labor law in the mid-1990s, there would be no more legislative initiatives around the issue. Supporters of labor in academia and legal circles stopped writing about the topic, focusing instead on the problems of organizing. Labor learned to bargain without the weapon of a strike by accepting concessions, moderating bargaining demands and using limited, and less effective, forms of strike activity. After a century and a half of struggle, the labor movement essentially abandoned the strike. The result, predictably, is a weak labor movement, unable to attract workers or to resist the erosion of what were once union strongholds.

THE PERSISTENCE OF THE STRIKE

Despite all the obstacles, workers at times still strike. Disregarding clear evidence to the contrary, some union officials persist in thinking that traditional methods can prevail. Sometimes, the union members dare to reject a contract, and the union business agent responds by handing them picket signs, declaring a strike and hoping for the best. With no strategy or organized campaign behind these strikes, however, they are doomed to failure. In other cases, workers strike because they feel they have no choice, such as at a Tyson poultry plant in Jefferson, Wisconsin in 2003. The workers at the plant resisted the company's demand for a four-year wage freeze, elimination of retiree medical benefits, and cuts to sick, vacation, health and overtime.[47] The employer's cuts were so intolerable that workers chose to fight rather than suffer under such draconian terms. Basically, Tyson was attempting to level the unionized plant down to the level of their non-unionized plants down south. Facing such drastic changes, the workers decided their only option was to fight back. Despite great solidarity from the town, the strikers lacked tactics capable of winning the strike. Eventually, they were permanently replaced.

Such strikes are both heartbreaking and inspirational. Heartbreaking because it is clear that the workers cannot win playing by the rules of a rigged game. Yet, at the same time, they are inspirational because the workers have the courage to take a stand despite the long odds against them. Ultimately, when the labor movement once again embraces winning tactics, this determination to fight will carry the day.

4. LABOR'S FAILED SEARCH FOR ALTERNATIVES TO THE STRIKE

With the production-halting strike becoming a relic of the past, union activists of the last twenty years have had to turn to other mechanisms to try to pressure employers during collective bargaining. Thus, we have seen the rise of strike "alternatives" such as the one day publicity strike, the corporate campaign, and the inside strategy.[1] Each strategy, while supposedly an attempt to revive trade unionism, instead adheres to a system that has been established over the past 75 years to guarantee labor's failure. Without the traditional tactics of solidarity and stopping production behind them, none of these strategies havd proven powerful enough to make an employer suffer economically. In many ways, these strategies are a reflection of the current state of the labor movement. Rather than putting forth bold ideas calculated to challenge the current system of labor relations in this country, contemporary trade unionists have instead adopted a philosophy of pragmatism, of making do with what the existing system offers, instead of trying to break free of that system, as traditional trade unionists once did.

Nonetheless, in recognizing the limitations of these tactics, we must still acknowledge how creative and refreshing they have been in an era of union busting and decline. They have kept alive the fighting spirit in the labor movement, particularly in situations where a traditional strike would have meant crushing defeat. Therefore, it is important that we review these tactics so that we can understand how the contemporary labor movement operates in the absence of the traditional strike, as well as to see how, despite being limited by significant strategic shortcomings, many trade unionists still burn with the passion of the 1930s.

ONE-DAY PUBLICITY STRIKES

In a one-day publicity strike, the union informs management that its workers will be going on strike, but will return to work in twenty-four hours. Due to the short duration of the "strike" and the advance notification of the return to work, there is no opportunity for the employer to permanently replace the strikers. However, due to their limited timeframe, one-day strikes have little impact on the operations of a company. Since the union announces its intention to strike in advance, the employer is typically able to make alternate arrangements to cover the work for the day that the workers are on strike.

The main goal of the one-day publicity strike is, as the name implies, publicity, as the union tries to bring public and media attention to the grievances of its workers. Consequently, one-day publicity strikes have generally been used against employers who are susceptible to public pressure. Frequent targets have included hospitals, universities, and public employers. Since one-day strikes are not as useful in industries that are relatively insulated from the public eye, they have not been utilized in manufacturing for the most part, although the International Union of Electronic, Electrical, Salaried, Machine and Furniture Workers (IUE) did conduct a two-day strike in 2005 against General Electric, over health care cost increases.[2]

Because most public employee strikes, by their very nature, are fundamentally public opinion strikes, one-day strikes have frequently been utilized in public employee negotiations. Unlike the typical private sector strike, a public employer typically saves money during a strike because they simply stop providing services, i.e. they close the motor vehicle office or stop picking up the garbage, saving money by not paying wages to strikers. The strike usually continues until community pressure demand that it be settled.*

In recent years, the one-day strike has been embraced as a major strategy initiative by the SEIU. Since the mid-1990s, the union, in its core health care sector, has essentially abandoned any strike other than the one-day publicity strike. By analyzing data on strikes maintained by the Federal Mediation and Conciliation Service, one can see that while the SEIU engaged in frequent strikes of one to two weeks or more throughout the 1980s and early 1990s, the strategy virtually disappeared after that, to be replaced by the one-day publicity strike.[3]

SEIU's use of the one-day strike illustrates both the pros and the cons of the strategy. On the one hand, it has allowed SEIU to apply pressure in situations where an open-ended strike would have allowed employers to permanently replace the lower skilled healthcare workers that the union represents. In addition, the one-day strike has allowed membership participation in the bargaining process beyond mere picketing or rallies. However, despite the limited good that the one-day publicity strike does, what does it mean for the labor movement when one of the largest unions in the country has all but abandoned the traditional strike? In adopting a tactic that cannot produce significant gains for workers, the SEIU has essentially surrendered. At their best, the one-day strike supplies the illusion of struggle, distracting

---

*Public employee strikes are governed by state laws which vary greatly on restrictions on strike activity; in many states collective bargaining is not allowed, while in others, such as New York, the right to strike by public employees is limited.

from the real problems facing the labor movement, which is the lack of an effective traditional strike.

INSIDE STRATEGY: WORKING TO RULE

Working to rule, also known as the inside strategy, is based on employees strictly following the employer's own rules in order to impact production. As described in *A Troublemaker's Handbook II*, "Working to rule is not exactly the same as a slowdown and it is not sabotage, neither of which are legally protected union activities. Working to rule generally means restricting output, undermining quality, or cutting back on service by working strictly by the book."[4] By using the employer's rules against them, the workers attempt to control the plant from the inside.

A great example of working to rule was the 2003 campaign waged by the Communications Workers of America (CWA) against Verizon.[5] With the company hiring 30,000 replacement workers in preparation for a strike, the CWA realized that it needed a radical strategy to keep its workers from losing their jobs. Thus, right before the strike deadline, the union announced that it would stay on the job and keep negotiating. Employees then followed Verizon's work rules to the letter, such as delaying "the start of their days with a 20-minute truck safety check" or refusing "to use fire escapes, which forced management to find other ways to gain access to phone boxes." After a month of working without a contract, the working to rule strategy, combined with a simultaneous campaign to mobilize public support, prompted Verizon to settle. The union was able to beat back management's attempts to force concessions, winning what one official called a "defensive victory."

Like other strategies discussed here, working to rule has proven able to supplement, but not replace, a strike that stops production. There are also limitations on how far the union can push the strategy without it being deemed a slowdown. Furthermore, if the activities continue after the expiration of a contract, the employer can legally impose the concessions they were seeking during bargaining once the negotiations are at an impasse. While the inside strategy belongs in any trade unionist's toolbox, because of its many inherent weaknesses, it cannot take the place of a traditional strike.

CORPORATE CAMPAIGNS

In a corporate campaign, unions pressure employers by a variety of means, including legal and regulatory challenges, boycotts, forming alliances with community groups, or by attacking business allies of a targeted employer. The idea is to hit the corporation from as many points of attack as possible.

By their very nature, corporate campaigns rely on a mixture of tactics. For example, one campaign might focus on interlocking boards of directors, while another might put more effort into pressuring suppliers.* For instance, during the *Detroit News* strike of the mid-1990s, "road warriors" followed members of the board of directors of the Gannet newspaper chain, owner of the newspaper, around the country, confronting them whenever the chance arose. During the Staley lockout in 1995, workers engaged in a boycott of the "end user" of the struck product, which was corn syrup. Since it is obviously impossible to boycott a product like corn syrup, the workers instead targeted an end user that used the product, in this case Miller beer.

Compared to the ineffective strikes of the 1980s and 1990s,

---

* An excellent, in-depth discussion of the internal debate in one union over such strategies is recounted in *Staley: The Fight for a New American Labor Movement* by C J Hawking and Stephen Ashby. Another good account of a corporate campaign is Tom Juravich and Kate Bronfenbrenner's *Ravenswood: The Steelworker's Victory and the Revival of American Labor.*

the corporate campaign is a quantum leap forward, as rather than standing on dreary picket lines, waiting for scabs to take their jobs, strikers actually go after the company. Despite their advantages, however, even a well-run corporate campaign can only produce limited results. While, in certain instances, a corporate campaign has forced an employer back to the bargaining table, rarely has it produced outright victory for labor. Many tactics of the corporate campaign, while laudatory, have had negligible effect, such as targeting individuals of a corporation's board of directors, as in the *Detroit News* strike. While this provides fodder for some good publicity, it is unclear how getting a company to drop a member of its board of directors has much impact on the outcome of a strike.

Overall, the corporate campaign has proven unable to substitute for a traditional strike that cripples production. First, time is on the side of the employer. As we have seen, after one year of an economic strike, only scabs can vote in an NLRB election at a struck plant. That means an employer can wait one year, and then have the scabs vote the union out. Corporate campaigns also take a long time to get up and running, time a union often does not have. This is why they have generally worked better in a lockout or unfair labor practice strike, where the employer can only hire temporary replacement workers. Corporate campaigns are also very labor intensive and require a large commitment of resources from unions, which many are unable or unwilling to offer. (A notable exception is the Steelworkers union, which has been willing to spend millions of dollars on corporate campaigns). Finally, and most damaging, an employer is able to continue operations during a corporate campaign. The scabs enter the plant and the product keeps coming out. As labor writer Jane Slaughter noted in the early 1990s:

> ...a corporate campaign that targets the power structure is a valuable tactic, but it must be combined with

the ability to hurt the company's pocket book directly. … It also means—easier said than done—finding a way to keep the company from continuing production with scab labor. This requires the willingness to face injunctions and arrests and to ask allies to do the same."[6]

While the corporate campaign can, on occasion, work in conjunction with a strike strategy, it will never replace a strike that halts production.

THE REDEFINITION OF SUCCESS

Since successes are not a common occurrence for today's labor movement, many trade unionists are understandably eager to declare victory wherever possible. After all, to keep a fighting spirit alive requires some good news every now and then. Thus, just getting back to work after a strike without being permanently replaced is often heralded as a win. In one sense, there is nothing wrong with this, as those who fight back should be celebrated. And, to a certain degree, victory is relative. To workers facing the destruction of their union, beating back the worst of concessions can very much be a triumph.

However, a true revival of the labor movement requires a qualitatively different definition of victory. Keep in mind that settlements considered victories by today's weakened labor movement would have been bitter defeats several decades ago. As AFL-CIO President Richard Trumka declared at a conference, "we need to quit thinking not losing is winning." To attract new membership, unions must demonstrate the ability to improve worker's lives. That means returning to a definition of victory measured in absolute gains for working people, not just the beating back of concessions that employers try to force on unions. Simply put, half measures cannot revive the labor movement. Yes, a well run corporate campaign can get management to back off a bit. A one-day strike can win some tiny gains for workers. But, at the end of the day, these limited strategies are the strategies of defeat. They represent the notion that the labor movement must make do with small victories and weak tactics. After decades of decline, it is time to admit that these small-bore notions of victory are in truth defeating the labor movement.

EVERYTHING NEW IS OLD, AND NOT NECESSARILY BETTER

The more you study labor history, the more you discover that tactics that appear to be new are in fact just old tactics wrapped up in new packaging. One-day strikes, working to rule, even corporate campaigns are, in large part, less effective versions of traditional union tactics that have been modified and watered down to avoid running afoul of court decisions that have chipped away at the powerful strike of the first half of the twentieth century. For example, the predecessor to working to rule is the slowdown, which has a long history of use by labor. The Industrial Workers of the World called it "striking on the job." The one-day strike is an updated version of the intermittent strike, which was employed with great frequency in the late 1930s and 1940s, while the end user targeting of the corporate campaign draws upon the strengths of traditional solidarity boycotts.

Let us first discuss the tactical ancestor of the one-day strike, the quickie or intermittent strike. In an intermittent strike, a union struck for a short period of time, say for an hour or a day, went back to work, then struck again, repeating this pattern indefinitely. As is the case with the one-day strike, the short nature of the intermittent strike provided a defense against the employer's use of permanent replacement scabs, as management was unable to plan production or operate efficiently without knowing whether workers would strike or stay on the job. It also dramatically expressed rank-and-file power in the workplace, and, importantly, allowed workers to continue getting paid, except for the short period when they were striking. Quickie or intermittent strikes (and the related slowdown) particularly inflamed management because they would go to the heart of the company's ability to control the workplace at the point of production.

The power of the intermittent strike can be seen today in the airline industry, with CHAOS(TM). The acronym for Creating Havoc Around Our System, CHAOS was developed in response to the failed airline strikes of the 1980s, in particular the 1986 TWA strike in which thousands of flight attendants represented by the Independent Federation of Flight Attendants were permanently replaced. (Federal courts have held that intermittent strike activity is protected under the Railway Labor Act, so a union can engage in an intermittent strike of individual flights.) Unlike one-day strikes in other industries, CHAOS(TM) can inflict major economic harm upon an employer. The strategy relies on the consumer's concern that future strike activity will impact their travel plans. It is one of the few contemporary examples where workers can engage in a protected action that can also affect employer operations.[7]

However, very few private sector workers are covered under the Railway Labor Act and thus able to make use of tactics such as CHAOS(TM). For those who fall under the NLRA, different rules apply. In that case, the Supreme Court, in a series of decisions from the 1930s to the 1960s, ruled that intermittent strikes were unprotected under the NLRA.[8] In this context, "unprotected" means that while the courts have determined that it is legal for unions to engage in a certain activity, employers are free to legally terminate workers for engaging in said actions. As Craig Becker, a labor attorney recently appointed to the National Labor Relations Board by President Obama, pointed out in the mid-1990s:

> ... the law does not recognize a right to strike if the strike
> blurs the clear-cut boundary between working and stop-

ping work, a restriction that dramatically circumscribes the range of protected strike activity. In order to maintain the NLRA's protection while continuing to exert pressure on their employer, strikers must leave the workplace, wholly abandon their work, and remain on strike until a settlement is reached, the strike is broken, or the strikers as individuals cross the picket line. As a consequence, workers are constrained to wage a form of strike that leaves them highly vulnerable to permanent replacement."

Despite what the courts have ruled, intermittent strikes appear to be protected by the NLRA. The text of the Act states that concerted activity is protected and that it is an unfair labor practice for an employer to interfere with protected rights. According to Becker, the main rationale for the Supreme Court's position forbidding the intermittent strike was that "… intermittent strikes are too effective."[9] He notes that other courts have been even more explicit about this, such as the Ninth Circuit Court of Appeals, which "explained that partial and intermittent strikes are unprotected because they 'unreasonably interfere with the employer without placing any commensurate economic burden on the employees.'"[10] However, the effectiveness of an action should not be the determining factor on whether or not it should be protected. Overall, the court decisions against intermittent strikes are the continuation of more than a half-century of judicial bias against labor.

SOCIAL UNIONISM AND THE ABANDONMENT OF THE STRIKE

In recent years, social unionism has become the preferred path to trade union renewal for many progressives. Advocates of this philosophy argue that labor must form coalitions with other groups so that together, they can advance their common interests. Social unionists reject a narrow focus on collective bargaining at an individual plant, arguing that unions must speak for all workers, not just a privileged few. Because of this expansive worldview, they support activities such as living wage campaigns, raising the minimum wage, and the labor/environmentalist "blue-green" alliances. Proponents of social unionism point to grassroots activism such as workers centers and community labor coalition as the best way forward for the labor movement. Indeed, some of the most vibrant activism in the labor movement today comes out of the social union model.

The problem with social unionism is that labor/community ties and coalitions, while important in their own right, are not a replacement for direct struggle against employers. In social unionism, the strike is abandoned, and in the process, the central role of workers at the point of production is lost. Although appearing progressive, social unionism in fact represents a shift in power from workers to union officials and non-profit staff, who are engaging in most of the outreach. Social unionists also sidestep the key economic concerns that must be at the center of labor's revival, namely that any trade union strategy must be capable of redistributing wealth and power. While organization and broad social ties are important, in and of themselves, they do not put food on the table for workers.

At the core of any union strategy must be the question of power. Despite what social unionists believe, organization and community ties alone do not lead to power. Rather, they must be coupled with tactics that can improve people's lives by taking income from employers and distributing it back to workers. There are two ways to do this. One is through collective action in the form of a strike. The other is by influencing government to act on behalf of workers. Social unionists opt for relying on government intervention instead of direct action by workers. While some gains can be made in this way, there are clear limits to what government can and will do for workers.

In criticizing social unionism as a strategy for the labor movement, I am not criticizing the often creative activism used by its adherents. Those who advocate for worker centers and living wage campaigns are not necessarily claiming to provide a new path for the entire labor movement. Instead, they are trying to organize particular groups of workers, and doing some very good work realizing meaningful gains, in particular for low-wage workers. As the labor movement creates new forms of organization to wage the struggles necessary to revive trade unionism, the social union paradigm will prove to be invaluable. However, in the current climate, the abandonment of the workplace—and by extension the strike—are fatal failures of social unionism.

Two books published in recent years advocate a social union approach. Examining these books will help demonstrate the limits of the social unionist agenda. In *A New New Deal: How Regional Activism Will Reshape the Labor Movement*, Amy Dean argues that regional labor bodies can transform the labor movement.[11] Dean lists three steps to regional power building: developing a regional policy agenda, forming deep coalitions, and building aggressive political action. Among the examples she uses to support her theories are campaigns to make sure employers receiving public subsidies pay a living wage to their workers, ensuring that development projects benefit the community, and pressuring government officials to support organizing efforts. Dean also discusses the building of community ties. All of these focus on getting local government—cities, counties, etc.—to influence employers.

Unfortunately, local government has little leverage against private employers, and that leverage is primarily limited to employers that pay low wages. Certainly, where local governments contract with private vendors for services, they can use the "power of the purse" to demand that those contractors pay a living wage. While important, these living wage campaigns touch only a small subset of employers, and are focused mainly on employers that pay near the minimum wage. For the vast majority of workers, whose employers are not susceptible to the threat of losing government contracts, social unionist campaigns offer little. Remarkably, Dean managed to write an entire book on the future of labor without talking about the strike. As her work shows, directly confronting corporate power is not on the social unionist's agenda.

Dan Clawson, in *The Next Upsurge: Labor and the New Social Movements*, argues that the key to labor's revival is for it "to form alliances with other social movements; for those groups, not employers, to have cultural and political momentum; for a mass movement, not staff, to be taking leadership."[12] While Clawson is accurate in noting that unions have grown during social upsurges and not in isolation from other societal forces, like Dean, he fails to explain how alliance building and restructuring translate into increased union power. Employers will not yield to employee demands unless workers have the means to impose significant costs on employers if their demands are not met. Clawson's discussion of living wage campaigns and other similar actions fail to define what those costs, if any, would be for employers. While many of his points are worthy of attention and incorporation into labor's overall strategy, they are not the recipe for an "upsurge" but rather the expansion of non-profit organizing, mostly staffed by middle class professionals, not workers.

Reading Dean and Clawson leads one to wonder exactly where workers fit into the social unionist agenda? If, as they believe, the path forward for the labor movement is building alliances with outside social forces, who exactly is going to carry those alliances out? From recent experience, it will most likely be the employees of central labor bodies and non-profit staff. This poses the question as to whether a workers' movement can be led by middle class reformers? In the great upsurges of the past, it was workers who were the creators of their own history, with ordinary men and women transforming society, and themselves, in the process. Traditionally, labor upsurges were characterized by strike waves in which millions of workers engaged companies in battles for control and power. The individual worker had significance only as a member of a vast congregation of workers. Thus, the massive rail confrontations of the 1800s, the 1934 general strikes, and the 1946 strike wave, to name just a few of many examples, all represented genuine social unionism, rooted in the workplace, broad-based and capable of changing society. That is what creates real and meaningful social change. Any social unionism not connected to the workplace is a false social unionism.

Therefore, to realize the goals of social unionism, labor needs to recover the tools of workplace-based solidarity and industry-wide confrontation, which actually do breed a broadened form of consciousness where workers can connect with larger, outside societal forces. As Rick Fantasia explains in *Cultures of Solidarity*, his excellent sociological analysis of strikes and organizing campaigns in the 1970s, the solidarity "the strike achieved and expressed was not inherent in the workforce, as some might romantically contend, but was to a significant degree a product of the collective action itself."[13] To Fantasia, the way to build solidarity is to engage in actions that build solidarity. This concept should be familiar to any competent workplace organizer. You start with a petition, move on to a ribbon campaign, followed by a march on the employer, and eventually, if need be, a strike, building solidarity every step of the way.

Strikes create broad social consciousness. For example, in the mid-1990s, during an intense labor conflict in Decatur, Illinois—which featured simultaneous strikes and lockouts by Staley, Caterpillar, and Bridgestone/Firestone—employees forged a shared solidarity, which was captured by union billboards that welcomed people to the "War Zone."[14] Likewise, in the mid-1980s, striking meatpackers at a Hormel meat processing plant in the rural community of Austin, Minnesota represented by United Food and Commercial (UFCW) Local P9 sponsored a mural on their union hall featuring Nelson Mandela. The mural read, "If blood be the price of their cursed wealth, then good God we have paid in full." The strikers did not start out being supporters of the South African liberation struggle, but in the course of their labor battle, they made connections with the larger anti-apartheid movement. In *Hard-pressed in the Heartland*, Peter Rachleff writes how

> At the beginning of the strike, a P-9 artist painted a map of the United States using a dot and a line to Austin to show the sources of solidarity. By the end of the strike, the map was so filled it was impossible to pick out lines or dots. More than 3000 local unions sent material assistance.[15]

These workers did not start out with an intention to join with a larger movement. Yet, in the process of their struggle, they developed a broader social consciousness. This is how a strike transforms participants. For those who have been part of one, this point should be clear. Leading up to a strike vote, it seems as if something is in the air. A group identity is forged or strengthened. Individuals make decisions they would not make on their own; people decide questions from a group identity perspective. Lines between labor and management become drawn.

In that regard, strikes are no different from other social upsurges. Strikes pull groups of workers together and in the process establish a new identity for the entire group. By collectively confronting their employers, workers challenge a system of workplace oppression. As a strategy, the strike is unrivaled in its grassroots, worker-centered character, in its ability to transform those involved, and in the direct confrontation with corporate power.

In contrast, the tactics of social unionism lack the immediacy of the strike, as its rallies and lobbying are far removed from the issues of the workplace.

PRAGMATIC LEFTISM AND THE DECLINE OF THE MODERN LABOR MOVEMENT

After the political fervor of the 1960s dimmed, many student and antiwar activists chose to enter the labor movement as a way to hold onto their progressive beliefs. For the next two decades, these former activists immersed themselves in union activities such as rank-and-file caucuses and shop floor struggles. By the early 1990s, many of these activists had risen to positions of influence as elected officers or union staff. Many of those who did not remain part of the labor movement drifted into academia, eventually populating labor education services and labor history departments. As a result, much of the leading ideas in the labor movement for the past twenty years—such as social unionism— have come from people who came of age politically during the 1960s.

Many of the changes that have come from this group has been welcome, including better positions on immigrants' rights, a critique of AFL-CIO foreign policy, and vastly improved union views on race and gender. None of these contributions should be underestimated. At the same time, despite their supposed progressive credentials, this group as a whole holds some of the most conservative beliefs in labor history on the questions of collective bargaining and strike theory. As a result, for the first time in the history of the American labor movement, there is near unanimity among policy makers and analysts that labor can survive without a production-halting strike. Indeed, with rare exceptions, one finds absolute silence on the chief question facing the labor movement—the decline of the strike.[16] How did the idea of the strike become so marginalized among those on the left of the labor movement?

Despite their background as part of the political and ideological left, the views pushed by many ex-1960s activists today demonstrate a remarkable pragmatism. During the late 1970s and 1980s, when many of these activists entered the labor establishment, the leadership of most international unions was intensely conservative and hostile to progressive ideas.[17] Working within a labor movement that lacked an aggressive or cohesive left wing, many formerly progressive policymakers accepted the new, management-centric order that was being created within the movement by the employer onslaught of the 1980s. Adapting their own ideas to match this new conservative reality, these activists created the one-day strike, the corporate campaign, and social unionism—tactics that functioned comfortably within the existing structures imposed by management and the legal system. As a result, for the past two decades, many of these "progressives" have been essentially pushing a pragmatic, non-confrontational agenda, whose main ideas can be summed up as follows:

1. Unions must only fight within the bounds of the law
2. Workers and the workplace are not at the center of the struggle
3. Middle-class progressive staffers know more than workers and thus should take a lead role in union strategy
4. Progressive union staffers do not have different material interests than rank-and-file workers
5. Building organization, rather than confronting management, should be labor's main mission
6. One can accept the fundamentals of capitalism and still devise effective trade union tactics
7. Ultimately, workers must rely on the power of the government in order to make gains

8. Militancy is naïve and should be marginalized
9. To argue that unions need to break free from the current labor system is too radical

Taken together, these ideas amount to an extremely conservative philosophy of trade unionism, a philosophy that would have been summarily rejected by previous generations of union leaders, on the left and right.

To be clear, not all progressives in the labor movement subscribe to the ideas listed above. Important countercurrents do exist. The point here is not to pick on the activist sector of the labor movement or on social unionism advocates. Quite the opposite, as the activist/progressive wing of the labor movement must play a vital role in any revival of trade unionism. However, as long as those on the left of the labor movement continue to lead trade unionists down ineffective, pragmatic paths, the movement as a whole will never be able to reinvent itself.

BUSINESS UNIONISM

During the 1970s and 1980s, many on the left of the labor movement advanced a critique of what is called "business unionism." Instead of concentrating on social-themed issues such as working conditions, distribution of profits, and fairness and justice, business unionism "focuses largely on bread and butter issues, economic questions of wage and fringe benefits."[18] In business unionism, decision-making comes not from rank-and-file workers, but is "built around a centralized administration and powerful leadership," with unions operating like service providers or extensions of the employer's human resources department.

The primary problem with business unionism is that it creates a system where union officers and staff are, in essence, separate from the members they represent. This separation allows an informal kind of corruption to flourish, where union staff and officers may have fancy cars and high salaries, but little connection to the rank-and-file, and therefore no real incentive to work hard on behalf of their membership. The gulf between the rank-and-file and full time staff has become a major problem of the contemporary labor movement.

In most unions, the staff member assigned to bargaining (known variously as the business agent or staff bargainer) has an inordinately dominant role in the outcome of the collective bargaining process. Possessing the "technical expertise" that rank-and-file members supposedly lack, the staff bargainer has significant control over union resources, and often relates to management representatives independently from the membership. Because of this distance from the rank-and-file, what for a worker on a bargaining committee may be an urgent struggle over a stalled contract can become just one of many files sitting on the staff bargainer's desk. What to a shop steward is a direct and personal fight with a supervisor at the worksite is, for a business agent, just one of countless grievances awaiting arbitration. Even during the bargaining process, instead of pushing management for the best deal for workers, in many cases, the staff bargainer plays a conservative role, favoring settlement and compromise over fighting to maximize the best possible gains for the rank-and-file.

There are a number of systematic conditions that encourage this type of behavior. First, business agents and full time officers do not experience oppression in the same way or to the same extent as do the workers they represent. For anyone who has been a rank-and-file leader and then gone on to become a full time officer, the difference should be clear. Most union staff jobs are far better than the jobs that rank-and-file members have, as pay, vacation, sick and health benefits for union staff usually far exceed what most workers receive. Beyond that, union staffers do not have to punch in a time clock or do repetitive work.

Furthermore, a business agent often has greater material incentives to settle a contract rather than engage management in a protracted fight. Most immediately, failing to settle a contract and, instead, pursuing a tactic such as a strike means much more work for union staff. However, there is no bonus pay for fighting harder, and no extra rewards for going on strike. In addition, a strike or other action not protected by current labor law can put the financial viability of the union at risk. A crushed strike could mean a loss of revenue from striking members' dues, with union staff facing the loss of their jobs. Moreover, to actually win a strike, a union may need to violate injunctions, subjecting them to potentially enormous fines that could lead to bankruptcy. All of this leads towards cautious behavior on the part of union officials, whose livelihood depends on the rank-and-file staying on the job and not striking.

None of this is to say that all union staff or officers are bad people, or that rank-and-file members are pure and if only they were in charge, things would dramatically change for the better. In fact, the problems facing the labor movement are deep-seated and structural, and go far beyond merely replacing one set of leaders with another. Unions must act together on a class struggle basis—which requires new strategies, new tactics, and a new ideology. Unfortunately, many unions believe that the best way forward is to centralize decision-making, ala the business unionism model. It is unclear why they believe, in the absence of evidence to the contrary, that those far removed from the workplace are the best ones to drive the struggle forward.

MILITANCY AND THE UNION DEMOCRACY MOVEMENT

Standing opposed to business unionism is a militant trend within the labor movement that opposes union bureaucratization and seeks to make unions more democratic and worker-centric. One of the best-known examples of this trend is Teamsters for a

Democratic Union, which since the 1970s has sought to rid the Teamsters of corruption and push for a more aggressive stand against employers. Along the same lines, organizations such as the Association for Union Democracy, based in Brooklyn, New York, seek to educate rank-and-file members about their rights. This reform movement has contributed greatly to trade unionism in recent decades, as dedicated rank-and-file activists have fought to end corruption, introduce greater competency, and prompt reluctant union officials to fight back.

This agitation has made a real difference, with many of the bright spots of the last several decades being the fruits of the struggle for union democracy. Thus, the Teamster strike at UPS in 1997 would not have happened without the decades-long battle to reform the Teamsters, which ultimately led to the election of reformer Ron Carey as President. Similarly, the Pittston strike in the early 1990s, led by Richard Trumka, likely would not have occurred—or been as militant as it was—were it not for the Miners for Democracy reform efforts in the 1960s and 1970s.

Yet, union democracy movements, by themselves, will not transform the trade union movement. To become a powerful, fighting force, unions need to develop new ways of thinking, new tactics and new structures. Business unionism is not the result of immoral union officials, but rather the natural consequence of a particular method of trade unionism where newly elected union reformers face the same conditions as those they replaced. As Bill Fletcher and Fernando Gapasin write in *Solidarity Divided*,

> The "misleaders" then are not akin to seaweed, floating forever on the ocean with no roots. They are more like crabgrass, which is deeply rooted and durable. These leaders' roots are not just in one section of the base but in the overall culture and practice of the organization.[19]

These problems are inherent in a system of trade unionism based on exclusive representation and job control.[20] That is why organizations such as Teamsters for a Democratic Union have linked the fight for union democracy with demands for militancy during national contract bargaining. In one of the few books on the labor movement to focus specifically on union democracy, Mike Parker and Martha Gruelle, in *Democracy is Power: Rebuilding Unions From the Bottom Up*, note the connection between democratic functioning and the ability to fight back against management:

> But far from being a distraction, internal democracy is key to union power. First, a union will act in the interests of members only if those members control the union. If members do not control their union, then others tend to run it in their own interests—management, the mob, or officials seeking to preserve their easy job and comfortable lifestyle if not line their own pockets....Second, the power of the union lies in the participation of its members, and it requires democracy to make members want to be involved.[21]

Gruelle and Parker discuss the difficulties not only in reforming unions, but also in unions functioning effectively once reformers gain office so they do not merely replicate the conditions that gave rise to business unionism in the first place.

Lacking a comprehensive strategy to beat back employer offensives, however, reformers these days can do little more than struggle to be administrators of unions trapped within the current, narrow labor system. Certainly, reformers can be more honest or competent than the incumbents they replaced in office. A progressive business agent who cares about workers' issues, returns phone calls, and fights hard is better than a burned out hack wanting to work as little as possible and treating members as pests. However, at the end of the day, both are stuck within a system of declining union power and a multitude of legal constraints that force unions into compromise and concession in order to survive.

Ultimately, any proposal for trade union renewal must have the struggle for union democratic rights and militant leadership as its central goals. To engage in militant struggle, labor must reconnect with the grassroots, become willing to take risks, and reject the status quo. However, whether such "fighting organizations" can develop within the existing labor movement or will require new forms of worker organization remains an open question.

5. WHY ORGANIZING CANNOT SOLVE THE LABOR CRISIS

Concurrent with the decline of the strike over the past half century, the labor movement has also experienced a steep decline in union membership. From a peak of 35.7 percent of private sector workers in 1953, union membership shrank to 10.4 percent in 1995, on its way to a meager 6.9 percent of private sector workers by 2010.[1] Between 1985 and 1995, the United Autoworkers lost nearly 225,000 members, the Steelworkers 169,000 members, and the Teamsters 240,000.[2]

The main strategy that labor movement has engaged in to deal with its dwindling numbers is "organizing the unorganized." While this strategy appears straightforward—trying to bring previously unorganized workers into unions should theoretically increase union membership—in practice, the strategy has been a failure. In fact, the idea that the labor movement can resolve its crisis simply by adding new members—without a powerful strike in place—actually constitutes one of the greatest theoretical impediments to union revival.

The strategy of "organizing the unorganized" is rooted in the concept of "union density," which claims that unions gain power by increasing the percentage of employees that are organized in a given industry. The best expression of this position has been made by Stephen Lerner, an SEIU staffer. Lerner argues that organizing most of the employers in an industry decreases employer resistance to unionization. "Since union wages and benefits won't make them noncompetitive," he writes, "non-union employers have less rational business reasons to resist unionization if their competitors are unionized."[3] In the long run, according to Lerner, the only way for unions to guarantee stable collective bargaining is to organize all competitors within an industry. Otherwise, lower wage competitors will undercut the unionized firms, leading to loss of market share and eventual bankruptcy. That is why increasing density has traditionally been a cornerstone of union strategy.

While the latter part of Lerner's strategy is correct, he goes wrong when he reduces the problem of leveling wages in an industry to simply organizing that industry. In order to equalize wages within an industry, three factors need to be present: 1) the ability to organize a large portion of the industry (density); 2) the tools to bargain industry-wide (e.g. multi-employer bargaining, solidarity strikes, closed shop, pattern agreements); and 3) the ability to force the employer to agree to union demands (e.g., a strike without permanent replacement, effective tactics to stop production, workplace-based solidarity). Unfortunately, the union density model that Lerner champions addresses only one of these factors, the numbers of employers unionized in an industry, while failing to address the need for labor to possess the necessary tools to force an employer to reach an agreement. If labor wielded the economic tools of solidarity and stopping production—i.e. an effective strike—it would then be able to organize workers and achieve density. That is how the labor movement traditionally organized, and it was far more effective than today's methods. For example, when craft unions controlled the supply of labor in the nineteenth century, raising union density led to the equalizing of wages. Despite scattered examples like this, however, density has historically never been enough by itself to establish and enforce union standards on an industry.

Another weakness of the union density argument is how it treats labor markets. (A labor market refers to the pool of workers potentially available to be hired in a given industry). Lerner argues that, "The higher the percentage of an industry or labor market that is unionized, the greater the ability to take wages out of competition and raise standards."[4] However, even if an industry were fully organized, striking workers could still be replaced by workers from outside that industry. As a strategy, cornering the labor market has never worked for industrial workers, as they are too vulnerable to being replaced by other unskilled or semi-skilled industrial workers. This explains why a strategy based mainly on organizing alone cannot work. Just because a union has achieved density within a given set of employers does not mean that the union has density in a particular labor market, as the relevant labor market includes anyone available to be a strike-breaker. For unskilled workers, the pool of potential strikebreakers could be as large as the entire working class. For example, let us say that a union organized one hundred percent of the bus drivers in a metropolitan area. Striking workers would still face the problem of replacement by unemployed or underemployed workers from other industries or bus drivers from other cities. As striking Greyhound workers found out in the 1980s and early 1990s, employers had no problem finding scabs to replace them.

In reality, the theory of union density harkens back to a time prior to widespread industrialization, when craft workers could control the supply of skilled labor. Simply by cornering the market for skilled artisans, early trade unionists could command wage increases. With the onset of industrialization, the deskilling of work and the introduction of national labor and product markets, the time for that form of trade unionism has long since come and gone. Unions today simply cannot achieve high enough density to prevent scabs from taking the jobs of strikers, especially in an economy with permanently high structural unemployment. Thus, raising union density alone simply cannot produce higher wages or stable collective bargaining.

One could make an argument for a two-step process, wherein unions increase density and then take on employers. However, there are several problems with this approach. First, it has never been successful, as workers have never shown much interest in joining weak unions in the hopes of future gains. Workers do not join unions to build organization—they join unions to improve their employment conditions. In addition, this strategy merely delays resolving the underlying economic question of how to force concessions from employers. Eventually, labor must confront the issue of coming up with winning tactics.

Based on these factors, it is no surprise that the strategy of organizing the unorganized, which has become prevalent over the past fifteen years, has almost no success to show for its efforts and large financial expenditures. As Cornell University labor professor Richard Hurd points out, even so-called New Unity Partnership or "NUP" unions, which have demanded that the AFL-CIO restructure in order to organize, failed to make headway in their own industries. "But the fact remains," Hurd writes, "that even with Herculean reallocation of resources and substantial internal restructuring, the NUP unions have not been able to overcome these environmental forces to make major strides in their own markets on a national scale."[5] During the period many unions focused on organizing the unorganized, trade unions lost over 1.2 million private sector members, dropping from 9.4 million members in 1995 to 8.2 million members in 2008.

Most telling is the failure of the Service Employees International Union. According to an analysis sponsored by the SEIU itself, "the locals and the International combined spent $1.3 billion on organizing from 1997 to 2006."[6] On paper, SEIU's growth from this period looks impressive—from representing 1.1 million workers in 1996, when Andy Stern took office as president, to 2.1 million workers in 2009.[7] However, as labor author Steve Early writes,

> Some observers question whether the SEIU 'organizing model' is easily transferable to other fields...They note that SEIU has, until now, the singular advantage of operating mainly in the public sector, among smaller private sector firms, or within health care and home care entities which rely on public funding—a ready-made environment for union political leverage, lobbying and deal making.[8]

Indeed, if we examine the numbers more closely, we learn that most of SEIU's growth has come from two sources: mergers and the top-down organizing of home care workers, as from 1996 to 2007, the group gained 365,000 homecare and childcare workers.[9] These workers were not added through traditional organizing campaigns, however. According to the *Washington Post*,

> Many of the union's gains also came from deals cut with elected officials. For instance, the SEIU contributed $1.8 million to the campaigns of then-Illinois Gov. Rod Blagojevich (D), making it one of his top contributors. In 2006, he gave the union the go-ahead to organize about 20,000 home health-care workers.[10]

Mergers and raids of independent unions account for a large portion of the remaining 635,000. For example, SEIU acquired the 120,000 member Local 1199 in New York in 1998.[11] It has been estimated that between 1996 and 2007, SEIU gained about 350,000 new members through mergers and takeovers of independent unions.[12] This means that SEIU's traditional organizing strategy has actually resulted in essentially no growth in membership. Look at the numbers. Between 1996 and 2007, SEIU gained about 700,000 members.[13] If 350,000 came from mergers, and 350,000 came from home health top-down political efforts, where are the new members that were added through traditional organizing campaigns? Some, to be sure, replaced members lost through attrition. But, even if the estimates are off a bit, SEIU has had at best minimal growth through traditional organizing. What originally looked to be impressive turns out on close analysis to be negligible return for $1.3 billion.

Despite these massive expenditures, SEIU has failed to raise union density in its core jurisdictions, including health care, as overall union density in hospitals was lower in 2003 than in 1993.[14] According to an analysis by the UNITE-HERE Strategic Affairs department, SEIU still only represents 10 percent of hospital workers. In Indiana and Illinois, after fifteen years of organizing, the union represents only 7,000 hospital workers out of a potential 300,000.[15] The entire point of organizing the unorganized is to raise union density in a given industry. By that benchmark, the SEIU strategy has failed miserably.

Numbers aside, advocates of organizing the unorganized have never adequately explained how their strategy leads to a revival of union power. And, given that the trade union movement has spent billions on organizing over the last fifteen years, that failure of explanation is remarkable. Of course, at a common sense level, trade unions will obviously be stronger with more members rather than with less. However, the best way to know if an idea works is to try it out in the real world. After nearly two decades of real world efforts, we can conclusively say that organizing alone will not resolve the crisis in American labor.

EMPLOYER REPRESSION, EFCA AND THE FAILURE TO ORGANIZE

According to organizing advocates, one of the main obstacles to the success of their strategy is employer repression against workers attempting to form unions. A study conducted by the Center for Economic and Policy Research determined that "in 2007, the most recent year for which data is available, 30 percent of union election campaigns had an illegal firing."[16] The study concluded that

> Current law has given employers a powerful anti-union strategy: fire one or more prominent pro-union employees—typically workers most involved in organizing the union—with the hope of disrupting the internal workings of the organizing campaign, while intimidating the rest of the potential bargaining unit in advance of the NLRB-supervised election.[17]

Workplace repression against organizing efforts is certainly nothing new. During the heyday of the labor movement in the early part of the twentieth century, an entire industrial labor spy industry was created expressly for the purpose of preventing workers from organizing. By the 1930s, more than 200 agencies were offering spy services to employers, with business spending an estimated $80 million annually on industrial espionage.[18] During a two-year period alone in the mid-1930's, General Motors spent $994,000 on industrial spies. The spies' job was to report to management on union organizing efforts so that the employer would know which workers to target. Frequently, spies were able to gain top offices in union locals, with the aim of subverting the union. Thus, union organizing efforts have long been the target of management repression. However, during the height of the labor movement, workers were able to organize in spite of employer resistance.

What is different today is, backed by a half century of labor law that has become increasingly and aggressively anti-union, employers are permitted to close plants, crush futile strikes, refuse to bargain wage increases, and take whatever action they deem necessary to prevent union organization and elections. According to Kate Bronfenbrenner, Director of Labor Education Research at Cornell University, "employers threatened to close the plant in 57% of elections, discharged workers in 34%, and threatened to cut wages and benefits in 47% of elections."[19] Lacking an effective strike, and hamstrung by a legal system that is structurally anti-labor, trade unions today are unable to force major gains from employers, especially in newly organized groups. Because of this imbalance in power, employers can prevent workers from organizing merely by threatening to take action against them, because workers know that employers have the legal ability to back up those threats. Employers can and do fire workers for union organizing without repercussion. The employer can move the plant to Mexico. Until the labor movement devises a strategy to adequately address these underlying employer strengths, unions will have difficulty organizing workers in any kind of meaningful way.

Despite their numerous advantages, however, employers still have to convince workers that being in a union is not in their best interests. If workers believed that the benefits of unionization outweighed the risks involved, they would overcome employer resistance and join unions, just as workers did in previous generations. However, these days, in a time of diminishing wages and high unemployment, employers are persuading many workers to vote against unions. Though this may seem illogical, it should hardly be surprising, as the reason goes back to basic economics: to attract workers, unions must be able to provide financial benefits to their membership.

Labor economist Bruce Kaufman, in *The Economics of Labor Markets*, applies classical economic theory to explain the cost-benefit ratio of union membership.[20] According to Kaufman, the benefits of union membership include greater bargaining power, more equality at work, increased job security, and protection from the unilateral actions of management. The costs of membership, however, include union dues that can run $400-$500 per year, the risk of lost wages during a strike, the possible loss of employment due to plant closings, the fear of management retribution, and perceived loss of individualism. While there were few risks and great rewards for joining a union in the first half of the twentieth century, today, the benefit/reward calculation has reversed.

Consequently, organizing advocates must focus on what it will take to persuade workers that unions can advance their economic interests, help them gain power in the workplace, as well as attaining a better quality of life in general. History is instructive here. If workers actually believed that joining a union would be in their economic self-interest, they will eventually cut through employer pressure and form unions. As an example, let us say, during the 1950s, a grocery workers' union approached potential members at a non-union store to bring them under the area-wide contract covering all grocery workers in the city. If the workers signed on, they would then gain employer provided-health care, pensions, and wages far above what they were earning previously. In this case, the workers would face a relatively simple choice and make the rational economic decision to join the union. Even if the decision entailed some risk, the workers could weigh the substantial benefits against the risks involved. When workers today weigh those risks, however, they frequently choose to vote against unionization.

The labor movement has essentially acknowledged that its organizing strategy is not working by sponsoring the Employee Free Choice Act. EFCA would require the National Labor Relations Board to certify a union upon submission of cards—the so-called "card check" provision—from a majority of workers within a bargaining unit. The intent of EFCA is to take the employer out of the equation by speeding up the election process. Despite its flaws, EFCA still deserves the support of trade unionists. On a practical level, it would ease organizing and presumably lead to increasing the number of members in organized labor. More members strengthen the union movement, even if the problem of wringing concessions from employers remains to be solved. Additionally, at a level of principle, EFCA stands on firm ground, as employers should have no role in the process of union formation, which should be strictly a matter of worker self-organization. The passage of EFCA would also eliminate some sources of employer interference in the election process.

However, we should not overestimate how much the EFCA would really help unions. Based on examining similar rules in place in some parts of Canada, Richard Hurd states that "...if instead of a 20% increase in organizing success we make what we believe to be an unrealistically optimistic assumption of a 100% increase, over a ten year period in the private sector we project that union density would grow to 9.5%."[21] While that type of growth might stabilize the decline of union membership in the short term, it hardly represents the salvation of the labor movement. Furthermore, these calculations include the dubious assumption that unfriendly labor boards and courts will not thwart the intent of the EFCA. Based on the experience in Canada, when employers are able to delay quick, or snap, union elections, union success drops considerably. Julius Getman of the University of Texas School of Law, who has studied the restrictions on organizing for decades, notes that "the courts, rarely a friend of labor, would be particularly hostile to nonelection certification. One way that they could manifest their unhappiness would be to reject certification for what they concluded were inappropriate units."[22]

Even if EFCA passed, trade unions would still face the formidable problem of negotiating a first collective bargaining agreement for newly organized workers. According to Kate

Bronfenbrenner, "…in 2007 there were only 1,510 representation elections and only 58,376 workers gained representation through the NLRB. Even for those who do win the election, 52% are still without a contract a year later, and 37% are still without a contract two years after an election."[23] When over half of successful union certifications lead to no contract during the first year, it is not hard to see why workers would not be keen on joining a union.

In response to this problem, labor pushed for mandatory arbitration of first contracts as part of the Employee Free Choice Act. This is a momentous and potentially disastrous shift in position for the labor movement, which has long resisted mandatory arbitration on the basis that arbitrators cannot be trusted to grant awards favorable to workers. For example, in 2009, an arbitrator in Quebec forced Wal-Mart to agree to its first union contract in North America, but only gave the workers a wage increase of thirty cents an hour, enough to cover their union dues.[24] Ironically, arbitration has usually been the last refuge of employers facing a militant and determined union membership. For example, when Samuel Gompers lost the presidency of the AFL for one year in the mid-1890s, he regained office by outflanking his opponents on the issue of opposition to mandatory arbitration. In defeating John McBride and regaining the presidency, Gompers summed up his anti-arbitration position by stating, "there was no one who stood so unequivocally against compulsion."[25]

MILITANCY AND UNION GROWTH

Historically, the fight for improving workers lives has been inseparable from the push to build unions. In *The Next Upsurge, Labor and the New Social Movements*, Dan Clawson notes how unions advance in leaps and bound, not incrementally.[26] "Historically labor has not grown slowly, a little bit each year," he writes. "Most of the time unions are losing ground, once in a while labor takes off. From the mid-1930s on, in the stretch of a little more than a decade, the number of union members increased fourfold."[27] In the years immediately following World War I, workers engaged in one the greatest strike waves in U.S. history. Hundreds of thousands of workers struck in the great steel strike of 1919, while over 400,000 rail workers took part in the shopman's strike of 1922.

However, following the defeat of these strikes and a red scare which purged much of its left wing, the labor movement remained intensely conservative through the 1920s. During this time, trade unions were more interested in establishing banks and insurance companies to service their members than fighting employers. It was not until the 1930s, when labor again confronted capital using militant tactics such as mass picketing and sit-down strikes, that workers flocked back to the union movement.

When labor did rise up in the 1930s, it was often led by a minority of members in a shop pulling the reluctant majority forward. According to Sidney Fine, the definitive chronicler of the sit-down strikes in auto in the 1930s, "the sit-down was marvelously effective as an organizing device for a union like the UAW that had succeeded in organizing only a relatively small percentage of the automobile workers."[28] During the sit-down strike in Flint, Michigan in 1937, union activists from one department fanned out through plant Chevy Number 4, where "A few staunchest unionists got into the aisles and began marching around crying 'Strike is on! Come on and help us!' A lot of the men kept working or made a desperate effort to do so. But the ranks of the strikers grew steadily as courage added to courage."[29] Soon, the workers had control of the plant.

In *The Emergence of a UAW Local, 1936-1939*, Peter Friedlander describes the process of forming a union in one auto parts plant in Detroit in 1930.[30] Here again, support for the union developed during the course of the struggle. Small victories such as an activist facing down a supervisor led to more members joining the union, which in turn led to more advanced actions. In a crucial move, the members of one department marched through the plant wearing union buttons. That is how labor organized back then, with a minority of workers pulling along their anxious coworkers through activism. Equally important, developments outside of the plant, such as the massive sit-down strikes, improved the morale of management and workers. As late as the 1970s, "'cultures of solidarity' were constructed by workers" in the course of their struggles against management.[31]

As these examples show, solidarity develops as part of a process. For anyone who has gone through a strike, this phenomenon is not hard to explain. In the process of striking, the workforce develops a group consciousness. The most militant workers pull along their hesitant co-workers. This prompts people to do things they might not do as individuals. Ultimately, this is how large social movements are built. In contrast, a system of organizing through government-sponsored elections demobilizes workers, as employees vote in the abstract for a union at an arbitrary snapshot in time, with no momentum behind their activities.

Forming a union is a collective action by its very nature, as workers join together to advance their common goals. Today, however, the decision to form a union is considered a choice best left up to the individual, in isolation from his or her fellow workers. This raises several problems. First, people don't necessarily make the same decisions as individuals that they would as part of a group. Second, approaching unionization as an individual decision requires workers to approach employers from a position of weakness, as labor's greatest strength comes in numbers—in the solidarity of workers acting together. Finally, the labor movement has historically approached the question of unionization on an industry or class basis, and did not leave the decision to individual workers, who it feared would undercut union standards by taking actions against the collective good of the group.

MINORITY UNIONISM AND NEW THINKING

The crisis in labor today has prompted some theorists and activists to reexamine the crucial characteristics of a union and to look back to earlier forms of unionism. Law professor Clyde Summers wrote an article in the mid-1990s arguing that unionists should jettison the entire concept of exclusive representation, which he called "a uniquely American principle."[32] This idea, that unions do not need a majority of the workers in a shop in order to form a union, is known as "minority unionism."*

Over the past few decades, numerous efforts have been made to develop a strong minority unionism movement. For example, since the early 1980s, Black Workers for Justice has organized African American workers in North Carolina expressly for this purpose. Similarly, the Communication Workers of America (CWA) sponsored a minority at the NCR Corporation during the 1990s.[33] In many states where collective bargaining is not permitted for public employees, unions have organized workers in minority unions. Most recently, the Industrial Workers of the World formed a Starbucks Workers union in 2004.[34]

Advocates of minority unionism hearken back to a pre-NLRA version of trade unionism, where the union existed because of the self-organization of the workers involved, rather than as an entity authorized by the federal government. During the heyday of traditional trade unionism, a small group of workers would often secretly form a union, which other workers were recruited to join. When a critical mass was reached, the union would expand its activities. The nature and extent of membership was determined by the number of employees who were active or who paid

---

*This argument was expanded in book form by Charles Morris in *The Blue Eagle at Work: Reclaiming Democratic Rights in the American Workplace*.

dues, not by government elections and bargaining units. Trade unionists back then also understood that they needed to show that they could be victorious before workers would have enough confidence to join the union en masse.

Whether majority or minority, however, unions face the same problem: how to force an employer to make economic concessions. Without an effective, production-halting strike, advocates of minority unionism can do little more than engage in relatively weak public pressure campaigns against employers. While they have been able to win occasional victories—most notably in November 2010, when, after three years of struggle, the IWW as able to pressure Starbucks to award time and a half pay for employees who worked on Martin Luther King's birthday—advocates of minority unionism have not been able to alter the wage structure in an industry.[35] That is why, like conventional unionists, advocates of alternative forms of unionism must grapple with the central question of how to revive an effective strike if they truly want to change the status quo.

THE ORGANIZING STRATEGY AND THE ABANDONMENT OF THE STRIKE

After a decade of employer aggression, by the early 1990s, trade unionists were desperately searching for new methods to fight back against management. It seemed that, after years of retreat, many in labor were finally willing to draw a line in the sand. Local P9 in Austin, Minnesota combined picket line militancy with a call for nationwide solidarity to take on Hormel. The Communications Workers of America at NYNEX successfully defended employer-paid health care with roving pickets and massive membership mobilization. Miners lead by Richard Trumka engaged in a militant battle at Pittston Coal in West Virginia using tactics such as stopping traffic with jackrocks, mine takeovers, and expanding the strike despite a federal judge's injunctions. The Justice for Janitors struggle was raging in Los Angeles, and unlike later, highly choreographed SEIU struggles, this one had a solid rank-and-file approach.

At the same time, many union leaders were asking whether labor might be better off without the National Labor Relations Act. Looking at the restrictions placed upon unions, combined with the lack of protection offered workers, these leaders theorized that perhaps the labor movement would be better off with no labor law at all, rather than the restrictive, anti-union laws that were in place. Lane Kirkland, the conservative leader of the AFL-CIO, was quoted in the *New York Times* in 1989 as speculating that maybe the labor movement would be more successful functioning with the "law of the jungle." In a speech to journalists, Kirkland stated that, "'As between present law and no law, I'd prefer no law'…He lamented that the labor laws banned solidarity boycotts by workers supporting strikers and said, 'The law forces us to work on products manufactured by nonunion employees.'"[36] Richard Trumka, then head of the United Mineworkers of America, noted bluntly that "The labor laws in this country are formulated for labor to lose. And if you play by every one of those rules, you lose every time."[37] During the strike at Pittston Coal, Trumka put those words into action, producing a rare victory for employees and demonstrating the power of labor's twin tools of disrupting production and workplace-based solidarity.

Reviving an effective strike was at the forefront of the labor movement's legislative agenda as well in the early 1990s. In 1992 and 1994, labor pushed to amend federal law to bar permanent replacement of striking workers. On the academic front, supporters of labor zeroed in on the legal restrictions imposed on the right to strike. Law review articles appeared with titles such as the *Enervation of the Economic Strike* and *Better Than a Strike: Protecting New Forms of Collective Work Stoppages under the National Labor Relations Act*.[38] In these articles, labor lawyers and academics pushed for changes in labor law to restore the original promise of collective bargaining.

While many industrial unions favored legislation to revive the strike, Andy Stern, at the time the SEIU's organizing director, argued that the legislative focus should be on organizing. Eventually, without public discussion, led by its "progressive" wing, the labor movement abandoned the fight to regain an effective strike in favor of "organizing the unorganized." With the adoption of organizing as its chief strategy, many trade unionists came to believe that they had found the answer to labor's crisis. Rather than expanding on the militancy of the Pittston miners, trade unionists opted for the relatively calm waters of union organizing. Taking their cue from labor, friendly academics focused on topics related to organizing, studiously avoiding discussion of the strike. Going forward, the labor movement would no longer focus on regaining an effective strike, but instead would concentrate on organizing. This decision has sidetracked the movement for the past fifteen years.

Why did trade unionists drop reviving the strike in favor of organizing? As noted by Bill Fletcher and Fernando Gapasin in *Solidarity Divided*

> Proponents of the organizing model focused, for either tactical or ideological reasons, on the symptoms of the larger problem-lack of organizing and the corresponding union decline-rather than on the problem itself: the existing structure and function of U.S. trade unionism ....[39]

Rather than resolving the more difficult questions of how to combat the employer onslaught, union leaders instead decided to focus on attracting workers to a dying labor movement. In many ways, it was an easier path, as adopting the strategy of organizing did not require a fundamental restructuring of trade unions. While creating an organizing department required a shift in resources, this type of work pales in comparison to the internal changes demanded to engage in militant confrontations with employers. Segregated in organizing departments, trade unionists are not required to deal with the ugly reality of bargaining and representing workers in an era of union weakness.

Perhaps more importantly, any strategy based on labor militancy and reviving the strike would eventually require trade unions to engage in a fundamental self-critique, something the modern labor movement is not prone to doing. A path of militancy inevitably engenders conflict, and supporting such a path would have led progressive staffers or aspiring national union officials into direct conflict with the more conservative elements of the labor bureaucracy. This is the type of conflict that threatens careers. Instead, the seemingly "progressive" plan of organizing the unorganized allowed "leftist" union officials to feel good about what they were doing, and to keep their jobs.

Thus, instead of challenging the status quo, those on the left of the labor movement fit themselves within the bounds of the existing structures, seeing the organizing of workers as an end in itself. Fletcher and Gapasin call this "the 'ideologizing of organizing,' which holds that organizing workers into unions is, in and of itself, a progressive, if not revolutionary, action."[40] Adopting organizing as labor's most important goal meant that other tasks, such as reviving labor militancy, could be put on the back burner. Fletcher and Gapasin note that while the organizing model "was a step forward for reformers, it was based on a superficial (or at best, partial) diagnosis of the larger problems facing the union movement, perhaps because of self-censorship by the left wing of the union movement to avoid being Red-baited."[41] Rather than seriously analyzing the underpinnings of their program, labor theorists simply avoided examining the necessity of reviving the strike.

In the first decade of this century, the labor movement has lurched from bureaucratic restructuring, to amending labor law, to calls to abandon the workplace and collective bargaining entirely. The one theory not remotely under consideration is the only tactic historically proven to wrest concessions from employers— an effective strike. Imagine telling Samuel Gompers or Mother Jones or the Reuther brothers or Jimmy Hoffa that trade unions could exist without a strike. However, in the name of pragmatism, the "progressive" trade unionists of today have fit themselves into a decaying structure. On a deeper level, they have abandoned the goal of creating the type of labor movement capable of transforming society. That is the tragedy of their generation.

6. THE SYSTEM OF LABOR CONTROL

Laws, court decisions and labor relations practices constitute the "rules of the game" that govern the day-to-day reality of trade unions. In many ways, these rules are more important than the results of any particular union struggle. For, if a company is victorious in a labor dispute, it has won but a single battle. However, if management as a whole can shift the rules decisively in its favor, it will win every labor conflict. This is exactly what has happened over the last half century, as management has gradually "won the war" by changing the legal terrain on which management-labor conflicts are waged.

At the same time, trade unionists have enabled this management-centric view of labor control to take hold by allowing it to displace the worker-based ideology that was prevalent over the first half of the twentieth century. Not only has management succeeded in changing the rules of the game, it has also succeeded in altering labor's very way of thinking. What has developed as a result is today's "system of labor control."

I refer to current labor law as a "system of labor control" for several reasons. First, it is in fact an overall *system*, with the pieces fitting together as a comprehensive whole constructed to control labor strife. I also refer to it as a system of *control* because its primary purpose is to confine and limit labor's ability to fight back against employers. This system is not just the accumulation of mistaken or unfortunate legal decisions—the entire point of labor law today is to control workers. By viewing labor law as a comprehensive *system of labor control*, trade unionists can move past opposing particular decisions piecemeal to rejecting the entire system outright.

I have already discussed some of the components of the system of labor control in previous chapters: the outlawing of effective strike tactics, the rules allowing the permanent replacement of striking workers, and the hostility to worker solidarity. Underlying these practical issues, however, are some very pronounced notions about the proper role of unions in society and the workplace. A quarter of a century ago, James Atleson wrote an important book titled *Values and Assumptions in American Labor Law*. Reviewing roughly fifty years of legal decisions to determine how "the courts could consistently restrict the rights of employees to take concerted action when those rights were clearly and unequivocally set out in the National Labor Relations Act,"[1] Atleson discovered that the outcomes of many labor disputes were supported not by the text of the NLRA or the facts of the cases themselves, but instead were based on a set of pro-management "values and assumptions," which had no basis in actual law:

- The continuity of production must be maintained
- Employees, unless controlled, act irresponsibly
- Employees are of a lower status than management
- Management controls the workplace through property ownership
- Although the business can be seen as a common enterprise, employees can never be full partners
- The Supreme Court refers to values without referring to class, assuming a harmony of values between labor and capital

As these "assumptions" clearly reveal, the system of labor control represents more than just an accumulation of bad judicial decisions; at its core, it operates at the level of ideology, postulating a pro-management viewpoint that fundamentally differs from how workers view the world. Challenging this pro-management bias is a key to reviving trade unionism.

THE TRIUMPH OF MANAGEMENT

Just how did this management-based point of view become enshrined in labor law? Karl Klare, in a groundbreaking article from the early 1980s, "The Judicial Deradicalization of the Wagner Act," argues that while the NLRA was "perhaps the most radical piece of legislation ever enacted by the United States Congress," its intent was subverted by the judicial system soon after its passage, beginning with the 1937 Supreme Court decision in *National Labor Relations Board v. Jones & Laughlin Steel Corporation*.[2]

Jones and Laughlin, a Pennsylvania-based steel company, had terminated several employees after they had tried to form a union.[3] The company then refused the NLRB order to reinstate the workers, arguing that the NLRA was unconstitutional. In 1936 and 1937, while the case was working its way through the court system, employers throughout the country generally refused to follow the NLRA. Faced with lawlessness on the part of management, workers had no choice but to conduct collective bargaining on their own terms, leading to a massive explosion of militant strike activity during that period.

Eventually, the Supreme Court declared the NLRA constitutional, ruling that Congress had the right under the Commerce Clause of the Constitution to regulate labor relations. In its decision in *Jones and Laughlin*, the Court alluded to the importance of the ongoing strike wave, noting that, "Experience has abundantly demonstrated that the recognition of the right of employees to self-organization and to have representatives of their own choosing for the purpose of collective bargaining is often an essential condition of industrial peace."

Although the upholding of the NLRA was a victory for the labor movement, the Court still took great pains to reassure management that its interests would be protected, as the decision in *Jones and Laughlin* did not disrupt the employer's traditional power in the workplace. As Karl Klare notes, "The Court rejected any inference the law would inquire into the substantive justice of labor management relations or the wage bargain."[4] This pigeonholing of labor relations into narrow contract law is one of the main methods courts have used to de-radicalize the NLRA.

Following the *Jones and Laughlin* decision, other Supreme Court decisions of the late 1930s adopted a similarly constricted view of labor rights under the NLRA, including the *McKay Radio* decision on permanent replacement, and the *Fansteel* decision against sit-down striking. These decisions show how, from the earliest days of the NLRA, the Supreme Court has sought to reshape labor law in a narrow, employer-favored manner. Nowhere has this judicial conservatism been clearer than in the Supreme Court's stance on workplace-based solidarity. In "Unions, Solidarity, and Class: The Limits of Liberal Labor Law,"[5] law professor George Feldman details the unspoken concerns that motivate courts and policymakers to ban industry-wide strikes in an attempt to make labor disputes as narrow as possible:

> The first concern is that workers who act on the perception that their interests are intertwined with those of their class will tend to develop a view that challenges capitalism. The second is that in acting this way, workers will necessarily create organizations based on class—call them social unions—that have the potential social power to carry out this challenge.[6]

Feldman notes the militant and broad-based nature of labor struggles in the early 1930s, which evolved into major confrontations between the working class and employers. During these confrontations, politicians, courts, and workers were forced to choose sides not between employees of a given company and that company's management, but between workers and management in general. Feldman writes how these confrontations often turned violent, on a "scale approaching insurrectionary proportions, beyond the ability of local authorities to contain." In each case, it seemed that

> the spreading of the conflict far beyond its origins and the resultant disorder, as well as the increasing openness of large numbers of workers to radical ideas and leadership, were caused by employers' unwillingness to concede what were basically moderate demands, especially their refusal to recognize a union. The employers' recalcitrance, it was easy to believe, threatened not only economic recovery, but the survival of the American political and economic order.

Labor history is replete with these types of disputes, where what started as a confrontation at a single company exploded into a fierce battle pitting workers against the employers in a city, region, or even the nation. Similarly, a strike which began in a given industry would often spread to other related industries, or beyond. As an example, going back the late nineteenth century, what started out as a strike of Teamsters dockworkers in New Orleans in 1892 developed into a citywide confrontation for power when, in support of their fellow union members, 25,000 workers representing 49 unions affiliated with the AFL launched a 4-day general strike.[7] This process was to repeat itself many times, such as in the Seattle in general strike of 1919, the San Francisco and Minneapolis strikes of 1934 and the Oakland General Strike of 1946, in which 100,000 workers struck in support of 400 striking retail workers.

Back then, in the days before the current system of labor control was in place, workers were able to develop their own ideas of what constituted proper tactics, and their inclination was often to expand a strike to garner the support of other workers. Thus, strikers at one plant would march from plant to plant calling on other workers to join in. For instance, in the May Day Strike of 1886, employees in Milwaukee who were seeking an eight-hour workday marched to "the Falk Brewery, the only larger brewery not on strike, to prevent employees from going to work."[8] These workers felt that it was "no longer a matter between individual workers and employers, but rather a test of power between workers and employers as a whole."[9] Railway strikes, in particular, had an ability to spread beyond an individual employer into nationwide confrontations pitting entire communities against rail corporations.

A motivating factor in passing the National Labor Relations Act was to prevent these types of strikes from spreading, as employers and their allies in the government sought to use the NLRA to narrow the permissible scope of labor struggle. According to George Feldman, the hallmark of modern labor law is preventing multi-employer or regional disputes:

> The cases discussed here reflect the liberal doctrine that labor law protects unions only insofar as they limit their role to that of representative of the employees of an individual employer, and that the law will resist any union attempt to move beyond this limitation. That doctrine rejects protection when the underlying issue implicates the proper role of unions in American society.

Notably, Feldman concludes it was often the liberal appointees to the Supreme Court who were the most interested in confining labor disputes to a single employer.

With the passage of the National Labor Relations Act, and its subsequent narrowing by court decisions and congressional amendments, employers and the government were able to reign in strike activity. Instead of class struggles, strikes became disputes between employees and their employer. By limiting the playing field as it were, employers and the government were able to depoliticize strikes, which ultimately contributed to the current conservatism of the trade union movement.

Narrowing the scope of struggle also had the effect of minimizing labor's conceptions of what was possible. By tying workers to individual enterprises, employees become tied to the fates of the particular company they worked for and felt part of a larger struggle. As we have seen, workers who bargain and struggle on an industry wide basis develop broader conceptions of themselves and their role in society. Conversely, workers whose only bargaining experience is with a single plant or employer form a limited notion of their ability to band together with other workers to fight back against employers.

BUSINESS DECISIONS AND THE ANTI-UNION OFFENSIVE

A major aspect of the anti-union offensive of the last several decades has been a conscious employer strategy to use "business" decisions to avoid unionization. To undermine unions, corporations have utilized tactics such as shifting production to areas where unions are weak or non-existent, forming non-union subsidiaries of the same corporation, and subcontracting work to non-union sectors of a particular industry. While the form has varied, the goal has been the same—to destroy unions.

Employer decisions to transfer production are part of the

carefully crafted system of labor control, as corporations frequently choose the location of new plants or expanded production based on union strength in a given locality. In *The Transformation of American Industrial Relations*, Thomas Kochan writes that

> One of the key choices that surfaces as firms adjust to changing markets is whether to expand and modify existing facilities or open new "Greenfield" sites. The outcome of these choices exerted a profound effect on the level of unionization in partially organized companies in the 1960s and 1970s.[10]

Kochan points out that many companies in the 1960s and 1970s based their decision on where to locate new plants on avoiding or weakening unions, such as the "southern strategy" of privileging new construction primarily in the non-union south of the United States. As a result, "a significant non-union sector developed in virtually every situation" during that time.[11] The practice has continued abated to the present day. While employers use different tactics in different industries, their aim is always to weaken or eliminate the unionized workforce. In trucking, for example, the practice of "double breasting" contributed to the loss of Teamster strength in the 1980s. Double breasting entails opening a non-union subsidiary to compete with the main unionized firm. Work is then diverted to the non-union subsidiary, which pays lower wages. In the airline industry, major airlines distributed flying to "regional carriers," which in many cases paid low wages to their workers. In other industries, subcontracting has allowed the shift of formally unionized work to non-union employers, such as in auto, where manufacturers spun off work to lower wage, non-union parts manufacturers.

No matter how militant or creative a local union is, if an employer is legally permitted to use business maneuvers to avoid unionism, the employer will always triumph. If a plant is closed or moved, work subcontracted, or the mine sold and reopened as non-union, there is little that a union can do to fight back, as, legally, the business decisions of the company are solely in the hands of management. And, unrestrained by unions, corporations will always make decisions that benefit themselves and undermine workers.

To the traditional trade union movement, the fact that a company closed up shop and then reopened as a non-union employer did not allow the company to avoid unionization. Instead, the company would be branded as unfair and subject to a boycott or a refusal by union laborers to work at the non-union shop. The main issue back then was the strength of union tactics such as the solidarity boycott or strike, rather than the legal details of who owned the business. For example, during the dramatic growth of Teamster power in the 1930s, it made no difference to union organizers which company a truck driver worked for. Instead, what mattered was that the driver had a union card. Failure to produce a union card meant that the truck would not be unloaded or the freight transferred. In addition, faced with competition from owner-operators, the Teamsters pushed to convert them into employees who could become part of the union contract, as "Considerable pressure was also put on brokers, shippers and other to stop using individual owners."[12] Rather than treat the contracting out of work as an insurmountable hurdle, the traditional labor movement used solidarity tactics to deal with the problem.

Fast forward seventy-five years, and during the recent economic crisis, we saw many employers using the threat of moving the plant to force concessions out of unionized workers. In Wisconsin, major industrial employers such as Kohler Manufacturing, Harley-Davidson, and Mercury Marine all won steep concessions from their unionized workforces by threatening to move their plants. As labor analyst Roger Bybee noted, the use of such management tools "will eventually erode the gains built up over eight decades by the UAW's struggles, unless and until the workers discover some new means of regaining their leverage."[13]

However, to much of the labor movement today, employer decisions such as where to invest, whether to subcontract work or move a plant are treated as if they are the product of external forces, beyond the control of unions. In reality, such decisions are part of the system of labor control. Employers understand the importance of this issue to workers, which is why, in more than half of organizing campaigns, the main threat by management is to close the plant.[14] To revive trade unionism, labor need to challenge the "right" of employers to make such unilateral decisions. To do so requires more than just changing particular rules, however, but rather a wholesale rethinking of the role of labor in society and the right of workers to have a stake in businesses that their labor helped create.

Unfortunately, the Supreme Court has long sided with employers to cripple the hand of unions attempting to deal with the business decisions of management. As Clyde Summers noted back in 1979:

> Decisions to continue subcontracting, to close one of several plants, to build a new plant, to liquidate assets, to sell part or all of the enterprise, or to become part of a conglomerate are all decisions which may be more important to the employees than wages or hours of work. Nonetheless, the courts have held that employees have no right to be notified, no right to discuss, and no right to use their concerted efforts to affect these types of decisions.[15]

Here, it is instructive to revisit the Supreme Court's decision in 1965 in favor of Darlington, a vicious anti-union employer. In the mid-1950s, the American Textile Workers launched an organizing drive at Darlington Mills in South Carolina, which was owned by an extreme right-winger named Roger Milliken. Milliken told the workers that he would shut down the plant if they voted in a union election. Undaunted, the workers went ahead with their vote, the union won, and Milliken, true to his word, shut down the plant. However, the NLRB eventually found in favor of the workers, and the case wound its way up to the Supreme Court ten years later. As *Time Magazine* noted at the time, the stakes were high:

> The court's hottest case posed a particularly important question: Can an employer close a plant entirely to avoid unionization? The answer is vital to multiplant textile manufacturers who have moved South in search of low-wage and largely nonunion labor. It is equally vital to the Textile Workers Union of America, still trying to organize Southern mill hands.[16]

Ultimately, the Supreme Court dismissed the union's argument by stating that the idea that "a single businessman cannot choose to go out of business if he wants to would represent such a startling innovation that it should not be entertained without the clearest manifestation of legislative intent or unequivocal judicial precedent so construing the Labor Relations Act."[17] This decision is clearly in opposition to the wording of the NLRA, which states that it is against the law to retaliate against workers for exercising their rights. What could be greater retaliation than taking away a worker's job? To the Supreme Court, however, the mobility of capital trumps worker's rights. James Pope notes that

> Darlington has exerted an increasingly devastating impact on unions as technological advances have smoothed

the way for corporations to move their operations. As we have seen, companies are permitted to shut down facilities for retaliatory purposes without any regard for the rights of employees at the closed facilities; the only employees who count are those at the company's other, still-operating facilities.[18]

In a related fashion, the Court also ruled that when a new company purchases a unionized shop, that company is no longer bound to the agreements that the previous owner negotiated. This area of labor law is known as successorship law. A typical successorship clause states that, "This agreement shall be binding on any successor and assigns." Unions expended much effort at the bargaining table to get this clause, believing that the clear and unambiguous language would protect them. Yet, in a series of cases in the early 1970s, the Supreme Court ruled that since the new owner was not party to the labor agreement, it was not binding on them. Then to make matters worse, the Court ruled that, as a matter of federal law, the purchaser has no obligation to bargain with the union unless they choose to hire a majority of union members.[19] While judges are supposed to interpret the law, what they were doing here was setting policy to attain a specific result, namely the freeing of capital from the "constraints" of labor contracts.

The underlying assumption running through all these decisions is that workers have no interest in their place of employment beyond the wages they receive. An employee could work in a plant for thirty years, and, according to the courts, still have no recognizable legal interest in the company. Trade unionists simply cannot continue to accept this viewpoint, for it means that workers are nothing more than commodities, raw materials to be thrown away when an employer has no more use for them. To reject this viewpoint, however, requires directly confronting the anti-worker legal system in this country.

CHANGING THE SYSTEM OF LABOR CONTROL

During the first part of the twentieth century, the labor movement engaged in a concerted, multi-pronged attack on the role of the judiciary in setting labor policy. By striking in defiance of injunctions, openly criticizing judges, and stirring the consciences of liberal policy makers, trade unionists eventually created a sense of crisis in elite political and legal circles. As William Forbath points out, fancy theories of constitutional law may be easy to ignore, but "Large number of people committed to those interpretations in the face of state violence and prison terms are harder to ignore. Sometimes, only the later kind of tenacity can undermine the political elite's commitment to an existing order."[20] Forbath explains that because of widespread defiance by workers of anti-labor injunctions, combined with articulate theories of labor rights, "a growing portion of the nation's political elite would come to share labor's sense of constitutional crisis."[21]

Traditional trade unionists understood that they had little choice but to attack the political elite, in particular the judiciary, as most judges, who were the ones ultimately making the laws that affected labor, were drawn from the ranks of upper tier law schools and corporate law firms. As a result, their income, their way of life, and their class outlook was quite different from that of the workers their decisions affected. Writing in the 1920s, labor commentator John Fitch noted that

> In the first place, most judges come from the employing, or the leisure, or non-wage earning class....A majority of them, therefore have not had, at the time of entering law school, personal contact with many of the harsher problems of life, or those which are particularly characteristic of the wage earners.[22]

As is still the case today, the path to becoming a judge was not based on representing poor or working people. As Fitch wrote of judges, "He will not have been a leader of forlorn hopes, nor will he have interested himself too much in unpopular causes not yet fully established."[23]

Thus, the traditional labor movement realized that it could not simply rely on judges to issue rulings that were favorable to workers, as those judges, for the most part, were far removed in social class from the daily struggles of labor.

Today, after nearly eight decades of post-NLRA legal decisions from both Republican and Democratic judicial appointees, it is time for contemporary trade unionists to acknowledge what their predecessors understood all too well: that most judges are anti-worker. While today's trade unionists have had no trouble recognizing the clear anti-worker bias present in the judicial appointees of conservative presidents such as Ronald Reagan and George W. Bush, many fail to see that Democratic-appointed judges are no friends of working people either. While Democratic appointees may differ from their Republican counterparts on issues that reside on the periphery of labor law, such as whether graduate students are eligible to join unions, on the questions paramount to the labor movement—whether unions should be allowed to engage in effective strike tactics, the mobility of capital, and the outlawing of solidarity—one finds little disagreement among judges, no matter their party affiliation.

Because of this, the system of labor control cannot be altered simply by electing new politicians, or appointing different judges. While a worker friendly government administration can influence labor law around the margins, merely electing Democrats instead of Republicans will not change the basic rules of bargaining. For example, consider what current legal provisions would have to change so that workers in this country would again have a real right to strike:

1. The principle established in *Mackay Radio* allowing permanent replacement of workers would have to be overturned.
2. The legislative rules banning solidarity activity would need to be repealed and industry-wide bargaining would once again need to be mandatory for employers.
3. Restrictions against union tactics that stop production would need to be undone so that strikes could be economically effective.
4. Unions would need the ability to bargain over basic business decisions, preventing employers from moving plants or playing shell games with corporate ownership.

None of these changes is even remotely on the horizon, no matter the party is in power. The labor movement is terminally ill, and anything that so-called "friendly" Democrats do short of the above measures amounts to mere hospice care, simply making the death of the movement a bit less painful.

Moreover, there is no evidence that Democratic judicial appointees are even interested in altering the fundamentals of labor policy. Federal judges, and in particular, those who make it to the Federal Courts of Appeals and Supreme Court, are not drawn from the ranks of progressive lawyers. Whether appointed by Democrats or Republicans, they tend, at best, to be corporate liberals sympathetic to the arguments of business. They are not the sort to wrench the steering wheel solidly in labor's direction by reversing Supreme Court decisions reaching back a half century. Here is what Jackson Lewis, the leading union-busting law firm in the nation, had to say about Sonia Sotomayor, President Obama's first appointment to the Supreme Court:

While Judge Sotomayor has more experience in the area of labor and employment law than other recent Supreme Court appointees, her record does not, as some might expect, place her on the pro-employee end of the spectrum. Given the number of pro-employer decisions she has issued over the years, she appears to take a flexible approach to labor and employment law cases. Based on this record, her appointment would not suggest a significant shift in the Supreme Court's disposition of these cases should she join the Court.[24]

Even in the unlikely event that the Supreme Court were to reconsider many of its past labor decisions, it is highly unlikely that Democratic appointees to the Court could be counted on to make the sharp turn in labor policy necessary to restore the right to engage in effective strike tactics.

Nor can changing membership of the National Labor Relations Board help the labor movement, as members of the board operate within the existing framework, and Democratic appointees have shown no inclination to radically change direction. And, even if they were, their rulings are subject to review by the federal courts. At best, while the NLRB can help with issues on the margins of collective bargaining, it lacks the power to fundamentally alter the system of labor control. No matter how pro-labor they might be, NLRB members still operate as administrators of an unjust system.

What will it take then to change the system of labor control? AFL-CIO President Richard Trumka offered one answer to the question back in 1987, when he was the newly elected reform President of the Mineworkers Union:

I say abolish the act. Abolish the affirmative protections of labor that is promises but does not deliver as well as the secondary boycott provisions that hamstring labor at every turn. Deregulate. Labor lawyers will then go to juries and not to that gulag of section 7 rights—the Reagan NLRB. Unions will no longer foster the false expectations attendant to the use of the Board process and will be compelled to make more fundamental appeals to workers. These appeals will inevitably have social and political dimensions beyond the workplace. That is the price we pay, as a society for perverting the dream of the progressives and abandoning the rule of law in labor relations.[25]

Unfortunately, Trumka's call for abolition was rhetorical, as no one in the labor movement—then or now—seriously considered proposing legislation to repeal the NLRA. And, with trade unionists unable to pass even the relatively minor provisions of the Employee Free Choice Act, there is no chance of passing the far more radical changes required to make the NLRA effective.

Without government action as an option, there is really only one way forward for the labor movement, and that is to repeal the NLRA by non-compliance, as a precursor to breaking free of the system of labor control. Obviously, this is not an easy path or one that will happen overnight, as dismantling the system of labor control will have to be a long term, strategic and coordinated project.

The first thing that labor activists will need to do is to launch a direct attack on the system itself, led by the left wing of the labor movement. As long as the most active and progressive elements of labor remain mired in confusion, engaging in half measures, there will be no one to challenge the current system. For there to be true change, the labor left must take the lead in developing a new theory of labor rights so that trade unionists can again believe—intensely—in the right to strike. This means developing firm and widely held principles supporting the use of effective strike tactics, as well as new forms of worker organization able to carry out such struggle. While this kind of confrontation may be uncomfortable for a movement long used to compromise, the alternative—muddling along or pursuing "safe" alternatives—will result in the destruction of what remains of the labor movement.

CONFRONTING GLOBAL CORPORATIONS

An important component of the system of labor control has been the establishment of the globalized economy, or "globalization," wherein unions confront massive corporations that have the ability to shift production throughout the world. While globalization has long meant different things to different people—as Kim Moody notes, the word "was typically an amorphous, all-encompassing analytical device that frequently concealed more than it explained."[26]—to the labor movement, it refers to the breakdown of trade barriers, the ability of capital to transfer work around the world, and the erosion of union standards worldwide. To some in the labor movement, globalization is considered inevitable, as technology causes national economies to expand beyond their borders. Yet, as noted by former AFL-CIO President John Sweeney, "This global order is neither a force of nature, nor the inevitable product of technology. It has been forged by governments, envisioned by conservative ideologues and enforced by corporate muscle."[27]

Globalization poses several difficulties beyond those faced by unions in the domestic economy. First, the discrepancy in wages between workers in the United States and those in "Third World" countries is so great that it creates problems in trying to develop worker solidarity. For example, if workers in the United States are making twenty dollars an hour and corporations can shift their jobs to another country where workers are earning two dollars an hour, it will undermine trade unionism in the United States, the higher wage country. In addition, while capital is able to roam the globe, labor unions are largely confined to national boundaries. With a worldwide market, establishing uniformity across all employers becomes difficult because global corporations are able to play workers and governments off one another.

This leaves the labor movement with a limited number of ways to confront globalization. One way is to try to protect higher wage labor markets by restricting imports. In fact, that was the initial response of the trade union movement in the 1980s. For example, when the U.S. auto industry came under assault from the import of lower cost Toyotas in the early 1980s, unions responded with appeals to U.S. nationalism in an attempt to persuade consumers not to purchase Japanese automobiles. Rather than devising a strategy capable of combating capital, the United Autoworkers instead fostered racist xenophobia, as groups of angry autoworkers would bash Toyota cars with baseball bats. Ultimately, the attacks degenerated into the exact opposite of the international worker solidarity required to confront global corporations. The level of venom reached such heights that a Chinese-American man in Detroit, Vincent Chen, was beaten to death by autoworkers in 1982 who believed he was Japanese and somehow to blame for the loss of their jobs.[28]

The other way to address imbalances in labor markets is to raise the pay of lower-wage workers. This means actively supporting the struggles of workers in the Third World to establish genuine trade unionism. However, the AFL-CIO, for most of the last half century, has pursued the opposite policy, more interested in advancing the policy aims of the United States government (and corporations) than in supporting real trade unionism. True solidarity requires a labor movement capable of joining with partners around the world to take on global corporations. As noted by Bill Fletcher and Fernando Gapasin in *Solidarity Divided*,

> The US labor movement needs to hold up its part of the tent. If manufacturing workers in the United States do not organize, growing unions in the Global South will lack the key U.S. allies they need to forge solidarity in the larger fight against global capital as well as the fight against specific sectors of manufacturing capital.[29]

Trade unionists need to envision a world where labor's conception of striking prevails over that of management. Otherwise, labor can only construct a solidarity grounded in weakness. As Kim Moody writes, "Crafting a strategy to deal with the changing economic world cannot be reduced to linking together today's existing labor movements in some formal sense. Linking together the walking wounded seldom wins a battle."[30] Clearly, today's weak strike has no chance of affecting global corporations. The real question is whether a strike based on stopping production and international workplace-based solidarity could successfully combat global corporations. This would require joint strikes against employers around the world. Unions could go after the supply or distribution chains of major union busting corporations using solidarity boycotts and solidarity strikes. The obvious problem is creating such a labor movement.

It is, however, a necessity. Instead of facing a single, domestically based company, unions today are often up against huge conglomerates, which operate in dozens of countries around the world. In this scenario, even if a union successfully employs militant tactics against an employer and shuts down production at a given plant, the employer can still outlast the union, as the production or profits from one plant may represent a drop in the bucket for many major international corporations.

However, this issue is not a new one for the labor movement, as trade unionists in previous generations also did battle against giant corporations. During the 1930s, unions took on massive corporations, many of which rival the size of those that unions face today. General Motors was not simply 'big', but as *Fortune* remarked, it was "colossal." It had sixty-nine automotive plants in thirty five cities and fourteen states"[31] as well as 171,711 hourly employees.[32] To combat a company of this size, the then fledgling UAW approached organizing at General Motors as but one battle in an overall war. For example, the sit-down strike in Flint was but one part of a series of strikes to organize the entire corporation. To traditional trade unionists, a single strike was but part of a larger strategy to organize an entire company or industry.

Going back even further, historian Lloyd Ulman notes the difficulties unions faced during the late 1800s and early 1900s in establishing stable collective bargaining in industries dominated by large corporations. Among the problems that Ulman listed were "the relatively low degree of skill required of the large firm's employees; the staying power of the big concern; [and] the facility with which a small number of firms can coordinate their strategy."[33] Ulman also wrote about the "multiple plant problem." If two plants were owned by separate corporations, striking and stopping production at one plant would put pressure on the owner because of the potential loss of business to his competitor. But, as Ulman writes, "if these two plants are controlled by the same interests, and one of them is shut down, production may be diverted from the idle plant to the plant remaining in operation."[34] Traditional trade unionists understood that they could not win a single battle against a company that owned more than one plant. To those trade unionists, it made little sense to take on only part of a giant corporation. Unlike today's unions, they instead typically struck the entire corporations at once. Reflecting this strategy, one of the early craft unions in the steel industry had in its constitution that, "Should one mill in a combine or trust have a difficulty, all mills in said combine or trust shall cease work until such grievance is settled."[35]

In contrast, in the 1980s and 1990s, unions often struck a single part of a massive corporation, with generally disastrous results. For example, despite spirited picket lines, massive rallies, and success at causing a drop in circulation, the 1995 strike against the *Detroit News* still failed, as strikers were up against a giant media corporation, Gannet, which was large enough to absorb the losses from a single striking paper. Even if the strikers had successfully stopped the newspaper from functioning (which they did not), Gannet would still have had no problem outlasting the work stoppage, as the company was not reliant solely on the income from the *Detroit News*. Rather than showing that the strike is an inadequate tactic in today's labor wars, however, the *Detroit News* strike showed only how a particular form of striking—namely hitting a small part of a large corporation—cannot work in today's world.

The problem, then, is not the size of the corporation, but a question of union tactics. As Ulman wrote, "In 1907 Samuel Gompers claimed that, 'Organized labor has less difficulty dealing with large firms and corporations today than with many individual employers or small firms.'"[36] The ease of entrance into the market, the lower capital required and the stiff competition generally prevailing in the industry make standardizing wages difficult in industries with many small employers. Different tactics are required to successfully establish collective bargaining, depending on the characteristics of the industry. So once again, the problem becomes not the impossibility of victory, but the inadequacy of modern union tactics. Therefore, the inability to tackle large corporations must be seen as a problem with the specific form of strike activity employed today, rather than some intrinsic weakness of the strike in general.

7. THE PRINCIPLES OF LABOR RIGHTS

To have a chance to win strikes again, the labor movement must challenge the unilateral "right" of employers to run "their" businesses without worker involvement. An effective strike—one which blockades the plant or chokes off a company's supply chain—by its very nature interferes with an employer's ability to run their company. Therefore, a union movement that challenges the mobility of capital must contest the right of employers to unilaterally make business decisions.

In order to do this, trade unionists must break with the dominant, management-inspired viewpoint of the last three decades by rejecting many of the fundamental notions of "free market" economics. The reason is simple: If labor accepts management's views on the role of workers in production, or how company resources are accumulated and allocated, then it is impossible to justify necessary and legitimate trade union tactics. Instead, labor must develop a working class perspective that establishes a set of principles that clearly justify the refusal to follow unjust and illegitimate restrictions on the right to strike. As legal scholar James Pope explains, concise, morally grounded principles can "mobilize supporters, stiffen their resolve, justify confrontational and even illegal tactics, and signal elites that workers were fighting over issues of fundamental principle...."[1]

In trying to establish these principles, trade unionists have much to learn, ironically, from the efforts of right wing political activists in the United States. Pope notes, for example, how advocates for gun rights have developed theories of constitutionality based on their own set of beliefs and principals, which are often in opposition to the rulings of courts and politicians. The National Rifle Association's website states that its mission is "to preserve and defend the U.S. Constitution, especially the inalienable right to keep and bear arms guaranteed by the Second Amendment."[2] Advocates for gun rights fervently believe they are fighting over matters of fundamental principle, not mere changes in policy. Whether or not one agrees that NRA members are defending inalienable rights is beside the point; the crucial fact is that the group is able to use its own internal ideology to motivate its supporters.

Gun rights advocates are not unique in this, as many other social movements, both on the right and the left of the political spectrum, uphold what they consider to be a higher morality, and consider pronouncements by judges and politicians as mere opinions. For example, anti-choice forces refuse to accept the validity of the Supreme Court's decisions regarding abortion, convinced that government officials who support a woman's right to choose are morally bankrupt. An example even more on point is the civil rights movement of the 1960s, which practiced defiance of laws that it considered to be the illegitimate products of racist institutions. For those activists, greater principles were at stake; because of their unshakeable beliefs, the laws of this nation were ultimately changed.

Traditional trade unionists exhibited this same independence of judgment, often acting in defiance of the prevailing laws of the time. This wasn't a calculus based on political leanings, as even conservative labor officials of the early 1900s scorned anti-labor judicial rulings. In fact, just as many conservative activists do today, the labor leaders of seventy-five years ago articulated their own sets of rationales, often in opposition to the views of management and the legal system. As William Forbath notes in his illuminating book *Law and the Shaping of the Labor Movement*, "...labor activists expounded a competing language of rights. They claimed entitlements to jobs and workplaces as well as broad freedoms of action and association and immunities from state coercion."[3] While there certainly were differences within the labor movement over tactics, the movement as a whole upheld the right of workers to engage in an effective strike.

Unlike the contemporary labor movement, trade unionists of the past bitterly resisted restrictions on the right to strike, as "principled disobedience to injunctions was official AFL policy from the late 1880s until the passage of Norris LaGuardia and beyond."[4] One of the principles of the Industrial Workers of the World was that "Strikers are to disobey and treat with contempt all judicial injunctions."[5] Even conservative union leaders such as Samuel Gompers said things like, "Injunctions regarding industrial relations I hold to be illegal."[6] Gompers understood that these powers were beyond the scope of the courts, saying that, "Such injunctions can and ought to have no real authority. I believe that those to whom such injunctions are intended to apply ought to pay no attention to them whatsoever, but should stand upon their constitutional rights."[7]

It was labor's agitation, and more importantly, the open and principled defiance of judicial orders, that won workers the right to strike and stop production. William Forbath notes that trade unionists of the early 1900s violated the law even in the face of state violence and threat of imprisonment. "From the 1900s through the 1920s," he writes, "a widening campaign of massive and articulate defiance of the courts helped the labor movement win support for its exiled constitutional claims."[8]

During the critical decade of the 1930s, this same moral

certainty empowered labor to defy the power of the courts and the government. Trade unionists took over plants, stopped production with mass picket lines, and denounced employers who attempted to continue production. In addition, police who attempted to intervene in strikes by escorting scabs across picket lines were considered to be union-busters. It was the underlying belief that their actions were legitimate and that those who opposed them were in the wrong that allowed workers to engage in such militant action. For millions of working class Americans—meatpackers, truckers, autoworkers—the labor movement's defiance of the law in the 1930s made possible an entire way of life, just as defiance of the law ultimately accomplished desegregation, the dismantling of racist Jim Crow laws, and the gains of the civil rights movement.

"LABOR IS NOT A COMMODITY"

As discussed back in chapter 1, to management, human labor is simply a commodity—something to be bought and sold on the open market without regard to its specific origin. While employers will rarely say this aloud, it does sometimes slip out. During a strike against Motts, the apple juice maker, in 2010, Tim Budd, an employee of the bargaining team, heard a plant manager say across the bargaining table that employees were "a commodity like soybeans and oil, and the price of commodities go up and down."[9]

For the traditional labor movement, the notion that human beings were like objects, to be used up during the production process, was highly offensive. As Samuel Gompers melodramatically stated, "You cannot weigh the human soul in the same scales with a piece of pork. You cannot weigh the heart and soul of a child with the same scales upon with you weigh any commodity."[10] Traditional trade unionists believed that workers had rights unrelated to the price they could command on the open market for their labor. This view was supported by the Clayton Act, passed in 1914 after years of agitation by the labor movement, which contained the simple declaration that, "The labor of a human being is not a commodity or article of commerce."[11] When signing the Act into law, then President Woodrow Wilson declared that "a man's labor is not a commodity but a part of his life, and that, therefore, the courts must treat it as if it were a part of his life. I am sorry that there were any judges in the United States who had to be told that."[12]

As James Pope explains, the idea that labor is not a commodity is vital one for the labor movement, as it provides the intellectual justification for successful strike tactics:

> The treatment of labor as a commodity subject to the rules of the marketplace is a defining feature of capitalism. The claim of a constitutional right to strike—a right to interdict the free competition of individuals in the buying and selling of labor power— obviously imperiled the ideology and practice of commodity labor. The right to strike could not be justified without addressing the question of labor liberty per se.[13]

Well into the 1950s, labor leaders defended union activity based on the assertion that labor was not a commodity. For example, with employers complaining of national pattern or multi-employer agreements, and conservative members of Congress investigating whether labor unions were a monopoly, Arthur Goldberg, the legal counsel for the CIO and later a Supreme Court Justice, testified in 1955 that

> The charge that national or regional or pattern bargaining is "monopolistic" and "a restraint of trade" reverts, of course, to the basic fallacy that human labor is to be

treated as a commodity, and that organizations of those who have nothing to sell but the use of their minds and bodies constitute restraints of trade.[14]

Likewise, Walter Reuther, the leader of the United Autoworkers, testifying at a congressional hearing in 1953, bristled at the notion that labor could be considered a commodity:

> Well, you see, labor is not a commodity which you go and shop for in the free market place. Labor is something different than a commodity, and if you want to give American labor the status of another commodity you can go out and shop for on the free market place, you have missed the whole point."[15]

The fiery words of Goldberg and Reuther reveal the belief, held by generations of trade unionists, that treating labor as a commodity would undermine the very foundation of the labor movement, and lead to a number of conclusions favoring management. First, if labor is just like any other commodity, then it logically follows that the "free market" should determine the price of a worker's labor, just as it does with any other input into the production process. However, one of the main tenets of traditional trade unionism was that workers could not allow the market to determine wages and working conditions, as the market, unrestrained, will continually drive workers toward poverty, injury, and even death.

Part of the reason for this attitude was that traditional trade unionists had witnessed firsthand how the courts applied laws intended to regulate commerce to trade union activity. For example, while Congress passed the Sherman Antitrust Act in 1890 to regulate the power of massive corporations, the Courts soon subverted the intent of the Act, using it instead to justify sweeping injunctions against trade unionists, including an injunction in 1894 against Eugene Debs during the great Pullman railroad strike.[16] As Samuel Gompers said, "Labor power is a human attribute.... Both the injunction and the anti-trust law were intended to apply only to property. When courts put human labor power and commodities in the same category, they laid the foundation for serious injustice."[17]

If a worker's labor is treated like commerce, than it can be "sold" as with any other commodity, with management becoming the "owner" of that labor. Then, just as management owns a pile of lumber for example, once the purchase of human labor is complete, the employer would theoretically control the mind and body of the worker for the period of time they were on the job. Legal scholar Karl Klare expands on this idea, explaining how a labor contract is "more than a legal relationship" because it

> ...establishes an entire system of social relations in the workplace whereby the employer is entitled to control the worker's actions and choices during the major portions of his waking hours. Thus, labor contractualism functions as the institutional basis of domination in the workplace.[18]

To the extent that the labor movement accepts this "wage-bargain" as the natural order, the more difficult it becomes to justify the fight for power on the shop floor, as once the commodity (whether oil or pork or human labor) has been used in the production process, management becomes the owner of the final product. Once workers sell their labor, they have no further interest in the enterprise, as the employer now owns the final product and all profits derived from its sale.

Ultimately, the notion that human labor is not a commodity brings to the forefront the proposition that the rights of workers must trump market considerations. Whether one is arguing that courts cannot enjoin workers from striking, that bankruptcy law should not apply to labor contracts, or that unions should be able to monopolize labor markets, the phrase "labor is not a commodity" cuts through a host of employer arguments. On a deeper level, if the commodity status of labor is indispensable to a capitalist economy, then to say that human labor is not a commodity is quite radical in its implications. According to Karl Marx, wages were "a commodity which its possessor, the wage worker, sells to the capitalist. Why does he sell it? It is in order to live."[19] Thus, the rejection of the commodity status of human labor is also a rejection of the idea that the market should govern every sphere of human activity.

"LABOR CREATES ALL WEALTH"

Not only did traditional trade unionists reject the management viewpoint that workers were mere commodities, they in fact believed the opposite, that it was labor, not capital, who were the true creators of wealth. According to historian Lawrence Glickman, "the doctrine that 'labor creates all wealth' and that workers should therefore receive the 'full fruits of their labor' had broad support in nineteenth-century America"[20] In support of this belief, working class organizations of the time "endlessly repeated the claim that 'labor creates all wealth' and, accordingly, demanded that workers both receive their fair share of that wealth and that they play a central role in the governance of the republic."[21] For example, the Knights of Labor, the main national rival to the AFL during the late nineteenth century, was formed "to secure to the worker the full enjoyment of the wealth they create."

The idea that labor is the creator of wealth is best expressed by labor's famous anthem, "Solidarity Forever," which captures the basic unfairness of a system in which human labor is treated only as an input in the production process, with no rights to the enterprises it helped create:

It is we who plowed the prairies, built the cities where they trade;
Dug the mines and built workshops, endless miles of railroad laid.
Now we stand outcast and starving midst the wonders we have made,
but the union makes us strong.

The idea that workers had rights in their workplaces that were
equal to or exceeded the rights of management motivated union
activity during the 1930s. According to historian Sidney Fine,
during the sit-down strike at Flint, Michigan in 1937, the UAW

> ...contended that the strike was legal since the worker
> enjoyed a property right in his job, and in striking, was
> 'therefore protecting his private property—his right to a
> job.' The property right of the worker in his job, it was
> alleged, was superior to the right of the company to use
> its property as it saw fit since the workers had invested
> their lives in the plant whereas the stockholders of the
> company had invested only their dollars.[22]

As a group of sit-down strikers wrote Michigan Governor Murphy during the strike, "We are resolved to protect our rights to our jobs with our lives."[23]

Unfortunately, the opposite attitude exists today, as the media and many government officials tell us that it is in fact capital that invests in America and creates jobs. In truth, however, capital can create nothing without human labor. After all, capital cannot swing a hammer or change a bedpan. Capital cannot write a novel or drive a truck. One can have all the capital in the world, but without human labor, nothing will be created or produced. Ultimately, if one accepts the argument that labor has no right to that which it has created, it logically flows that once the worker has received his or her paycheck, the wage bargain is complete, and that worker has no further interest in his or her job. If traditional trade unionists had believed this, there would have been no point for the union movement to exist in the first place.

In recent years, the Harvard Union of Clerical and Technical Workers developed the slogan "Harvard Works Because We Do." As the slogan clearly points out, it is workers—the janitors, the food service employees, and the professors—that are the university. Without these workers, the university would be nothing more than a collection of buildings. Thus, by blockading a plant gate, disrupting a retail outlet, or conducting a sit-down strike, workers are taking back company property from the grip of management, and stating loudly and clearly that they have a powerful stake in the wealth that their labor has created.

"THE GLORIOUS LABOR AMENDMENT"

Traditional trade unionists also looked to the United States Constitution, and in particular the Thirteenth Amendment, to justify their right to strike. Passed after the Civil War to ban the last vestiges of slavery, the Thirteenth Amendment states that, "Neither slavery nor involuntary servitude, except as a punishment for crime whereof the party shall have been duly convicted, shall exist within the United States, or any place subject to their jurisdiction." Until the middle of the twentieth century, the Amendment—known back then as "The Glorious Labor Amendment"—"sustained workers' rights in much the same way that the Second Amendment supports gun rights today."[24] In If the Workers Took a Notion, Josiah Lambert argues that the right to strike became a limited commercial right under the NLRA rather than a more fundamental right based on the Bill of Rights or the anti-slavery amendments to the Constitution.[25] According to Lambert:

> Prior to the rise of the modern labor movement, labor leaders and reformers declared that the principle of free

labor supported labor protest—the right to strike was one of the liberties that distinguished the free worker from the slave and the bondsman. Strikes were not merely instruments for improving wages and working conditions but affirmations of personal autonomy and dignity.[26]

To some, the connection between union rights and involuntary servitude may seem to be a bit of a stretch. After all, if workers don't like their jobs, they can just quit and find another one, right? Yet, as legal scholar James Pope and union activists Peter Kellman and Ed Bruno note,

> In an economy dominated by large corporations, the right of a lone worker to quit offered nothing more than the opportunity to exchange one relation of servitude for another; either way, the worker ended up in servitude. Only by organizing, could workers rise above servitude. As CIO General Counsel Lee Pressman explained: 'The simple fact is that the right of individual workers to quit their jobs has meaning only when they may quit in concert, so that in their quitting or in their threat to quit they have a real bargaining strength.[27]

In other words, under the current system, what workers have the "right" to do is quit one bad job in the hopes of finding another bad job. However, true labor freedom requires strong unions capable of transforming bad jobs into good ones. Like the slogan "labor is not a commodity," the power in the involuntary servitude idea lies in the notion of labor freedom.

Whether one argues labor is not a commodity, looks to labor's traditional reliance on the Thirteenth Amendment, or attempts to revive the principles of "free labor," the underlying focus is the same: rejecting "free market" ideology in favor of trade union rights and ideals. Which particular variant is adopted is less important than that trade unionists begin to think in terms of fundamental rights for all workers.

PROGRESSIVE IDEAS AND THE LABOR MOVEMENT

When drawing on historical examples throughout this book, I have often looked to conservative trade union elements, rather than their progressive or radical counterparts. For example, I have used the more conservative American Federation of Labor rather than more radical alternatives such as the Industrial Workers of the World. I have also focused more intently on "conservative" leaders like Samuel Gompers. Similarly, rather than addressing the leading role of the Communist Party in many labor struggles of the 1930s, I instead choose to cite the more conservative CIO leaders.

The purpose on focusing on the more conservative elements of the traditional labor movement is two-fold. First, as Robert Fitch argues, "instead of the AFL, the direct institutional ancestor of most of today's unions, the new leftist historians would celebrate the AFL's more progressive but mostly defunct adversaries" such as the IWW, socialist Eugene Debs, or the early CIO.[28] Yet, in many ways, unions today are more like the conservative AFL than the radical IWW, and therefore, examining AFL philosophy is a better starting point to understanding today's union movement. In addition, it is often easy for modern trade unionists to dismiss the IWW or the radical unionists of the 1930s as historical relics, with no relevance for today's labor movement. I therefore hope that showing how, on questions of strike theory and economics, conservative trade unionists such as Samuel Gompers were more radical than even today's labor left, will force labor activists to question their ideas.

That being said, the importance of the left to trade union history cannot be overstated. In the 1930s, socialists, communists, anarchists and other radicals played key roles in leading many of the strikes we have discussed throughout this book. In fact, it is fair to say that the modern labor movement would not exist but for the effort of these leftists, who provided the militant leaders, radical ideas, and underlying philosophy that made possible the great gains of the movement in the first half of the twentieth century.

Unfortunately, many of these left leaning leaders were purged from the movement in the 1940s and 1950s. The main reason for this was one provisions of the 1947 Taft-Hartley Act, Section 9(h), which required trade unionists to sign affidavits saying that they were not members of the Communist Party. According to historian Nelson Lichtenstein, this provision sparked great controversy even among non-Communist labor officials:

> Even when taken at face value, section 9(h) did have a devastating impact on the unions. Initially, all trade union officials refused to sign the anti-Communist affidavits. Led by John L. Lewis of the AFL and Philip Murray of the Steelworkers, both labor federations indicated a refusal to sign, thereby severing relations with the NLRB and, in effect, nullifying the Taft-Hartley Law.[29]

Eventually, however, labor officials caved in, purging many leftists from the trade union movement in the process. This had the effect of eliminating some of the best trade union organizers from the movement. Even more importantly, this purge eliminated the very ideas underpinning the militant action that was responsible for labor's successes in the 1930s. As a result, ideas such as "labor is not a commodity" and "labor creates all wealth" were abandoned over the ensuing years in favor of a conservative position that considered unions to be in the business of selling labor and bargaining over the terms of those sales. When progressives finally crept back into the labor movement in the 1980s, most kept their left wing ideas in the closet, fitting their beliefs within the now dominant framework that accepted the superiority of capital over labor. By abandoning their ideals in the name of expediency, these trade unionists also abandoned the very ideas necessary for practical success.

8. LESSONS FROM THE STRUGGLE

For the labor movement to have any chance at reigniting the spark that was present back in the first part of the twentieth century, it must again develop into a fighting, grassroots force, capable of confronting corporate power. While many contemporary trade unionists continue to be stuck in a mindset that favors compromise and compliance over resistance and militancy, several labor conflicts of the last twenty-five years stand out for the tenacity of the union members involved, the level of rank-and-file activism, and the willingness to confront the system of labor control.

In four cases in particular—mineworkers at Pittston Coal, the "Charleston Five" long shore workers, factory workers at A.E. Staley and meatpackers at Hormel—employees faced an aggressive management determined to gut labor contracts and break the union. Unlike most trade unionists over the last three decades, however, these workers chose to take a stand, pushing the boundaries of labor law in the realization that simply playing by the rules of the game established under the system of labor control was a losing proposition. More recently, in 2008, workers at Republic Windows in Chicago inspired the nation when they responded to the closing of their plant with a bold tactic rarely used since the 1930s, a plant occupation. Trade unionists attempting to revive the strike must learn from these struggles if the labor movement is to have a future in this country as a force for worker rights.

PITTSTON COAL

If there was one labor/management conflict over the past quarter century that was infused with the spirit and militancy of the traditional labor movement, it was the battle the United Mineworkers of America (UMWA) waged in 1989 against Pittston Coal, based in southern Virginia. The stakes of this battle were high for the UMWA. In industry after industry, aggressive corporations had demolished pattern agreements during the 1980s, and Pittston appeared determined to do the same thing in the mining industry, refusing to sign on to the standard contract covering mine workers.

The UMWA immediately knew that Pittston's aggressive stance was a cause for concern, as the union had gone through a similar battle several years earlier with A.T Massey Coal in West Virginia after that company had also refused to sign on to the national contract, and instead insisted on negotiating with each mine separately. The ensuing strike was complicated and messy, involving injunctions against the union and attempts by the company to permanently replace the striking workers. In the end, the union was saved from likely defeat only when Massey was found guilty of unfair labor practices by the NRLB, prompting a compromise settlement to the strike. In the aftermath, the message to both employers and unions was that if a company were belligerent enough, it could impose its will on its employees, even in a union stronghold like West Virginia. From the Massey strike, the UMWA learned that a fundamentally different and more militant strategy would be required in future labor disputes.

By fighting a militant battle that at times went far outside the bounds of labor law, the mineworkers at Pittston were able to avoid the fate that befell millions of trade unionists in the 1980s and 1990s. Lead by Richard Trumka, before he went on to become president of the AFL-CIO, the Pittston struggle would ultimately show how a committed and unified international union with a militant membership and workers willing to disregard the restrictions of the system of labor control could fight back against a union busting company.

The Pittston strike went through several phases. During the initial phase, the UMWA, in a change from longstanding tradition, continued working even without a contract. This reflected the recognition by the union that tactical flexibility was required if they were going to have any chance at success. While the workers remained on the job, the UMWA engaged in a typical corporate campaign, attempting to put public pressure on Pittston Coal from a variety of angles. After a year of waging this campaign, it became apparent that the union was not generating enough pressure to force Pittston Coal to settle. On the contrary, the company was now threatening to impose a contract, and, to back up that threat, it began to hire scabs.[1] With the corporate campaign unable to force the company to back down, the union authorized a strike in 1989. In a wise move, the UMWA declared that the strike was over unfair labor practices, which, if upheld by the NLRB and the courts, would penalize Pittston Coal for hiring permanent replacement workers.

Once the strike began, the union engaged in legal picketing. However, Pittston went to court and obtained injunctions limiting the ability of the union to picket. If the UMWA had played by the typical script of the 1980s, it would have obeyed the judge, kept up a symbolic picket or two, and hoped that the unfair labor practice charges would eventually stick. Then, if they were lucky, the union members may have gone back to work with a concessionary settlement.

Instead, the UMWA opened up a new chapter in the struggle, characterized by non-violent civil disobedience. On April 18,

1989, the daughters of Mother Jones, a woman's support group named after the revered mineworker organizer from the turn of the last century, conducted a thirty-hour sit-in in the lobby of Pittston's headquarters in Lebanon, Virginia. At the same time, mineworkers and supporters began blockading roads leading into the plants. Thousands of strikers and supporters were arrested in these acts of civil disobedience, but the point had been made that the workers would not back down easily.

Pittston Coal then went back into court to try to get the union tactics enjoined. Not surprisingly, state and federal judges agreed with the company, imposing millions of dollars in fines on the union, and briefly jailing the strike leaders for contempt. In addition, ignoring the conduct of Pittston and its union-busting security force, Vance Security, (union members complained that Vance was instigating vandalism to make the union look bad, harassing union supporters, and even pointing rifles at striking workers), the judges instead bitterly denounced the mineworkers.[2] In response to the injunctions, the UMWA responded with strategic flexibility, backing off on certain tactics while opening up new fronts. In June, in response to the contempt citations for their larger civil disobedience actions, the mineworkers switched to smaller actions using convoys of vehicles to block roads leading into the mines.

It is important to note that at each stage of the struggle, the UMWA created a culture of solidarity among its members. For example, strikers adopted camouflage as their official clothing, which helped create group cohesion and fostered an identity of a militant unit of guerilla fighters up against a corporate behemoth. Additionally, with everyone wearing the same clothing, it was harder for Vance Security and the police to single out specific strikers. On nearby land, the strikers also opened Camp Solidarity, which housed thousands of supporters during the strike.

On September 17, 1989, the union upped the stakes when

ninety-eight miners and a member of the clergy dressed in camouflage entered the Pittston Coal treatment plant. They approached the security guards and informed them they were peacefully taking over the plant. Like the sit-down strikers of the 1930s, the miners were protected by thousands of strikers outside the plant.[3] Although the sit-down ended several days later, it was becoming clear that this struggle was going to be different then other union/management conflicts of the era.

The strike then entered into what can best be described as a period of rank-and-file lawlessness, with strikers and their supporters disabling cars using jackrocks, which are nails welded together so one side always faces up. As Richard Bribane explains in his book about the Pittston conflict, *A Strike Like No Other*:

> The lawbreaking also included the anonymous vandalism of Pittston, Vance APT, and private vehicles; rock throwing at vehicles belonging to company, guards, Pittston supervisors, and replacement workers; rocks thrown at and hitting the skid of a hovering state police helicopter; the extensive scattering of jackrocks, loose nails, plastic pipes studded with nails, and other devices to puncture hundreds of vehicle tires.[4]

In an attempt to spread the conflict, individuals wearing masks so they could not be identified began setting up picket lines at other mines in the area. This expanded the strike and put pressure on other mine owners and the government to intervene. While these actions were not officially sanctioned by the UMWA (and strikers alleged that some of vandalism was actually committed by Vance Security to tarnish the union), union officials did not condemn these tactics.

After nearly a year of struggle, the strike finally ended on February 20, 1990. Unlike other failed strikes of the 1980s and

1990s, the mineworkers had successfully resisted the concessions that management had been trying to impose upon them. In the end, they kept their fully employer paid health care, maintained their retirement benefits, and even secured a wage increase.[5] The Pittston miners had showed how, with membership mobilization and a refusal to play by rules that favored management, a union could win a strike in the modern era.

THE CHARLESTON 5

Another struggle that contains valuable lessons for today's labor movement is the case of the Charleston 5. In 2000, members of Local 1422 of the International Longshoreman's Association, a primarily African American local based in Charleston, South Carolina, waged a global campaign to beat back the prosecutions of five of their members stemming from a confrontation over scab labor. By developing a worldwide campaign to defend those five union members, Local 1422 demonstrated not only the power of worker solidarity, but also revealed how the only path to union victory is a refusal to follow the system of labor control.

The cause of the conflict was a decision by Nordena, a Danish shipping company, to break with decades of standard practice and use a non-union company to unload ships at the Port of Charleston. This was an obvious threat to the local union, since they knew that a non-union company could undermine union standards at the port. Initially, the local union members picketed whenever a Nordena ship came into port. After several months of engaging in this action and seeing no results, union members raised the level of protest, boarding a ship at one point. On January 19, 2000, matters came to a head. In a deliberate provocation, the authorities mobilized 550 police officers from law enforcement agencies across the state to do battle with the local. A confrontation ensued, which led to ten workers being injured, and eight being arrested.[6] Despite the fact that local officials and

Nordena wanted to resolve the matter, South Carolina Attorney General Charlie Condon, seizing upon the opportunity to bash a primarily African American union in the South, prosecuted the picketers.

In response, members of the local, led by President Ken Riley, built a national solidarity effort, raising hundreds of thousands of dollars for the arrested worker's defense fund. They eventually won the support of the national AFL-CIO, culminating in a rally in Charleston. Through their tireless efforts, Local 1422 build a powerful support network, with ties to dockworkers unions worldwide. The result was direct, immediate workplace-based solidarity at its finest, as long shore unions across the globe agreed to shut down ports on November 13, 2002, the day the workers' trials were to start. In the face of this demonstration of global union solidarity, the cases were settled the day before the threatened shutdown was to begin, with the felony charges dropped and the workers each agreeing to a misdemeanor with a $100 fine. Ultimately, Nordena also backed off from using a non-union firm to unload ships in the Port of Charleston.

By engaging in a militancy uncommon in the modern labor movement, Local 1422 was able to transcend the system of labor control to maintain union standards at the Port of Charleston. If the local had stayed within the bounds of the law, and contented itself with peaceful but ineffectual picketing, the Nordena

---

*Congress passed the WARN Act in 1988, and the law is supposed to provide advance notification of plant closings. However, employers routinely exploit loopholes in the law or just plain ignore it, as the penalties for violation are minimal. Every year, thousands of workers are cheated out of the notice and pay required under the WARN Act. According to an analysis by the Congressional General Accounting Office only one of nine workers facing mass layoffs or plant closing receive WARN notice. Even where it appears clear the employer should legally provide notice, they do so in only one third of the cases.

ships would have continued to unload with scab labor, and several union members would have ended up in jail. Instead, the union's militant actions set in motion a chain of events that produced a global network of workplace based solidarity that ultimately led to the settlement of the dispute in favor of the employees.

REPUBLIC WINDOWS AND DOORS

More recently, members of the United Electrical, Radio and Machine Workers of America (UE) demonstrated the power of strategically timed, militant action. In December 2008, with populist anger settling in across the country following the massive government bailout of Wall Street, for several days a small group of workers on the north side of Chicago captivated the nation. The workers, who were employed by Republic Windows and Doors, responded to management's plan to shut down their plant and deny them their severance pay with a dramatic action rarely seen since the 1930s—a plant occupation.[7]

On top of the closing, management was also going to shut down the plant on short notice, failing to comply with the sixty day notice requirements of the Worker Adjustment and Retraining Notification Act (WARN Act), a federal law meant to protect workers from sudden plant closings.* At the same time, workers at the plant suspected that management was secretly moving equipment out of the plant, after the local president, Armando Robles, discovered that the company was moving equipment out of the plant in the middle of the night. It subsequently came to light that management was operating a runaway plant, attempting to transfer the equipment to a new operation in Iowa. Eventually, the CEO of Republic Windows was indicted on charges of "looting the company and defrauding investors," something that likely would not have happened without the glare of the national media.[8]

Robles spoke with his staff representative, Mark Meinster,

to come up with a plan of action. Rather than a grievance or a lawsuit, they devised a bold tactic—a plant occupation. They then held a meeting with their workers, who enthusiastically supported the idea. The union decided to take over the plant on the last day of operations.

After holding the factory for six days, the workers forced the company to pay the severance owed to them by law. Faced with a similar situation, most unions would have either filed a grievance or lawsuit under the WARN Act, or gone to the NLRB to file some pointless charges over failure to bargain. However, the UE has always been a militant union. Billing itself as "the USA's Independent Rank and File Union" on its website, the UE proudly proclaims that "The Members Run This Union!" Indeed, several years earlier, workers at Republic Windows had thrown out another union, the Central States Joint Board, which had a history of labor racketeering and corruption, and voted in the UE.[9]

Strategically, during the occupation, the union kept its focus on Bank of America, who, "although flush with U.S. Government bailout cash, had refused to extend Republic's line of credit."[10] By adroitly exploiting public anger over the government bank bailout, the strikers were able to garner support from politicians, including then President-elect Obama. Ultimately, the importance of the plant occupation at Republic Windows was not just that the workers won the severance pay owed to them, but that they become a symbol of a militant response to the economic crisis, potentially inspiring workers across the country to think of new tactics to fight back against management.

While, unfortunately, the labor movement has failed to build upon the militant actions of the workers at Republic Windows, we can still draw a number of lessons from their struggle. One is that bold action can inspire many, and bring in support. The second is that when presented a plan involving personal risk, workers will respond if they see it as a path to justice. Third, militancy can be deployed in a controlled and strategic fashion, as the UE constantly kept the spotlight on Bank of America, the most politically vulnerable target. Finally, the struggle at Republic Windows shows the relationship between grassroots democracy and militancy.

STALEY AND HORMEL WORKERS ATTEMPT TO BREAK FREE FROM THE SYSTEM OF LABOR CONTROL

A pair of struggles that stand out because of the militancy of the workers involved and the solidarity developed during the conflict are the strikes of Local P9 of the United Food and Commercial Workers Union (UFCW) against Hormel in Austin, Minnesota in 1986, and the lockout of workers at A.E. Staley and Company in Decatur, Illinois in 1995. [11]

In the early 1900s, meatpacking was, as immortalized by Upton Sinclair in *The Jungle*, a difficult and brutal job. By the 1930s, little had changed in the industry. "Yet," according to labor activist Daniel Calamuci, "from the end of World War II until the1980s, meatpacking work came to be one of the better low-skilled manufacturing jobs in the United States."[12] Through collective bargaining, backed by an effective strike, workers won improvements in pay, working conditions, and safety, transforming meatpacking into an upper working class occupation.[13]

With the decline of the strike in the 1980s, and the rise of concessionary bargaining, the meatpacking industry began to witness a return to the type of conditions described in *The Jungle*. It was against this backdrop that Local P9 of the United Food and Commercial Workers in Austin, Minnesota decided to take a stand against the concessionary demands of the Hormel meatpacking company. The newly elected leadership of Local P9, interested in fighting rather than accommodation, hired labor consultant Ray Rogers in advance of negotiations. Destined to become one of the more controversial figures in the modern

American labor movement, Rogers was a strong proponent of the corporate campaign, promoting cross union solidarity and membership mobilization. Cutting his teeth on the Textile Workers Union of America battle against J.P Stephens in the 1970s, (a conflict that would become the model for the film *Norma Rae*), Rogers went on to form Corporate Campaigns, Inc., and would be involved in many important labor battles over the next several decades.

After Local P9 struck in August 1985, their confrontational stance attracted the support of trade unionists from around the country. Among the tactics the union engaged in was the corporate campaign—which it pioneered—utilizing road warriors who fanned out across the country, trying to expand the strike to other Hormel plants. In addition, when Hormel attempted to reopen the plant with permanent replacement scabs, hundreds of Local P9 supporters surrounded the plant.

Despite their militant efforts, however, Local P9 was ultimately undercut by the larger UFCW international union, which disagreed strongly with the aggressive strike tactics. For example, while Local P9 favored expanding the strike to other plants, the International was dead set against any attempts to broaden the conflict. In addition, Local P9 favored noisy demonstrations, confrontation with company officials, and angry press conferences, while the International was more comfortable with backroom negotiations. Most importantly, the Intentional did not even believe that Local P9 should be fighting the concessions. In contrast to Local P9's strategy of militancy, the international union's "strategy" was to control the pattern in the industry by negotiating concessions downward. The International argued that by granting concessions, it could preserve the wage patterns in the industry at lower levels. This proved to be a major mistake, as employers, recognizing union weakness, would continue to ask for more and more concessions over the following years. As a result of its increasing hostility to the local, the International eventually placed Local P9 in trusteeship, and settled the strike.

In the end, the most important thing about the P9 strike was the divide it revealed in the labor movement. On the one hand, Local P9's struggle garnered the fervent support of rank-and file workers across the country, inspiring thousands of trade unionists who wanted to see a more defiant labor movement emerge. On the other hand, the P9 gospel of militant solidarity, fierce independence from the international union, and willingness to skirt the edges of labor law made the group a pariah to many in the labor establishment. Even many progressive, mid-level officials lined up against P9, defending the international union's strategy of negotiating concessions.

Following the defeat of Local P9, wages in the meatpacking industry continued on a downward spiral. "Since the mid-1980s," writes Daniel Calamuci, "meatpacking has once again become a nightmarish workplace, as past gains for workers have disappeared. Wages in 2005 in some of the nation's largest plants dropped below wages in 1980 (in real dollars)."[14] While the strike was unsuccessful, even more damaging was the UFCW's policy of retreat and surrender.

Jump forward nearly a decade to another mid-sized Midwestern city, Decatur, Illinois. Heading into negotiations in 1992, workers at the A.E. Staley Company faced an ownership that seemed intent on forcing the union to strike. Like Local P9 at Hormel a few years earlier, the workers at Staley elected new leadership that was willing to engage in a fight. Rather than follow the typical labor script, the local decided to try some new tactics, including hiring Ray Rogers to conduct a corporate campaign. They also brought in Jerry Tucker, a former regional director and reformer in the UAW, to conduct an inside strategy.

On June 27, 1993, the Staley workers were locked out. In response, the union engaged in many of the tactics that had been pioneered by Local P9. For example, striking workers, dubbed "road warriors" traveled the nation, spreading the word of the strike to other trade unionists and building support for various boycotts. Solidarity committees also formed around the country, sponsoring actions in support of the locked out workers.

Eventually, after the Staley union, the Allied Industrial Workers, merged with the International Paper Workers union during the lockout, conflict developed between the local union and the international, just as had been the case with P9 several years earlier. Staley workers wanted "the UPIU to make the lockout a top priority by putting significant resources, both money and staff, into their fight. They wanted leadership of the sort that Mine Workers president Richard Trumka had exerted in the successful 1989-1990 Pittston strike."[15] Instead, they got an international union intent on ending the lockout, even if it meant accepting the employer's terms. After much in-fighting between the activists in the local and the international union reps, the international took over bargaining and settled the lockout in December 1995.

WHAT WE CAN LEARN FROM THE HORMEL STRIKE AND THE STALEY LOCKOUT

Along with the Pittston strike, Local P9's strike at Hormel and the Staley lockout represent the most concerted worker efforts of the past quarter century to break out of the system of labor control. As a result, any trade unionist looking to develop winning strike strategies needs to understand the tactics that these struggles used to achieve their aims.

Obviously, there are many similarities between the Staley and P9 conflicts. Both occurred in mid-sized Midwest cities. Both involved local unions fighting to keep long standing contractual provisions in place against newly aggressive employers. Both unions hired Ray Rogers and his Corporate Campaigns, Inc. Finally, both local unions eventually buckled against the pressure from their respective international unions to settle their disputes. Most importantly, however, these trade unionists rejected labor's predominant strategy of retrenchment and retreat. Instead, their answer to labor's decline was simple: to attempt to fight their way out of it.

Despite failing to achieve their objectives, the Staley and P9 battles proved that militant struggle was the only way forward for the labor movement. By fighting back against aggressive employers, the workers in each conflict transformed narrow disputes into larger battles that drew the support of trade unionists from around the country. In the process, both local unions developed into activist organizations, unleashing the creativity and initiative of their memberships. By contrast, while the Staley and Hormel workers were engaging in militant activity, hundreds of strikes were being lost in the 1980s and 1990s by unions married to the failed contemporary labor ideas of concession and retrenchment.

One cautionary lesson of the P9 and Staley conflicts is that any union that attempts to expand their disputes beyond the bounds of the current system of labor control will have to contend with others in the labor movement who are against this type of action. The Staley and P9 workers banged heads with their international unions, who in each case stepped in to settle the dispute, over the vociferous objections of the local union activists. This reveals the difficulty a local union faces in fighting a two front war against both the company and the international union. We will never know what could have happened at both Staley and Hormel if both locals had been supported by their international unions. However, as a basis of comparison, the Pittston strike, succeeded in large part because the militant actions of the local union were supported by the larger international union.

In addition to engaging in a militancy rarely seen in the labor movement today, the P9ers and Staley workers also brought a high level of worker solidarity to their struggles. By putting up picket lines at other plants in the Hormel chain, Local P9 drew the support of trade union locals from around the country, who joined with their union brethren despite the potential consequences. (When workers at the Hormel plant in Ottumwa, Iowa honored P9's picket lines, more than 500 of them were fired.[16]) Likewise, as we saw earlier in the book, the Staley workers joined with employees at Caterpillar and others to engage in an action reminiscent of the citywide struggles of the 1930s. Entering Decatur, Illinois during the lockout, billboards announced that you were entering "The War Zone." This showed how workers could use solidarity to make common cause against common enemies.

On the flip side, the Hormel and Staley struggles showed the difficulty of a single militant local union taking on a massive corporation one plant at a time. In contrast to the large-scale confrontations of previous generations, both local unions ostensibly fought their battles alone. No matter how militant a local union is on the picket line, we have seen how a large corporation can weather any work stoppage by either absorbing the losses or shifting production. That does not mean that fighting is bad or that a strike cannot prevail, but successful trade union strategy requires a corporate-wide approach.

Perhaps the most important lesson we can learn from the Staley and P9 struggles is that purely symbolic and sporadic civil disobedience are not sufficient. To prevail, labor must disrupt production. As evidenced throughout labor history, the factor most crucial to the success of a strike is "the extent of worker organization and the ability to stop production."[17] Ultimately, in both the Staley and Hormel conflicts, the local union was unable to stop production. While this was in large part due to the hostility from the international union, stopping production was never central to either union's strike theory, as both locals relied primarily on a corporate campaign strategy. Particularly at Hormel, Ray Roger's strategy of attacking business allies of the employer had limited success. Even if the international union had not stepped in to undermine the strike, the local union would still have needed to choke off production at the Hormel plant as well as figure out a way to expand the strike to other facilities.

Nonetheless, unlike most labor disputes today, both local unions did make at least symbolic attempts to disrupt the operations of the plant. At Staley, towards the end of the lockout, the local union engaged in civil disobedience, when on June 4, 1994, the one-year anniversary of the lockout, supporters blocked the plant gates. Forty-eight protesters were arrested, and the event gained widespread media coverage. Three weeks later, on June 25, the day of a major national rally, hundreds of strikers and supporters crossed the police line and were Maced by the Decatur police. After this, the local union decided to limit civil disobedience to purely symbolic acts.

Similarly, during the strike at Hormel, Local P9 engaged in several attempts to block the plant gate towards the end of the strike. When Hormel attempted to reopen the plant with scab labor on January 20, 1986, hundreds of activists in the Twin Cities joined striking workers in a picket and car blockade of the plant. Eventually, Democratic Governor Rudy Perpich called in the National Guard to act as strikebreakers and escort the scabs into the plant. After P9ers blocked the freeway going into town, the only cars allowed to travel were scabs with passes. Austin, Minnesota was a city effectively under martial law. In April, in conjunction with another national rally, hundreds of supporters again engaged in other disruptive actions at the plant gate.

While in both the Staley and Hormel disputes the attempts to stop production came relatively late in the game and were not sustained, even these sporadic attempts went far beyond what most other unions have done over the last two decades. While most contemporary unions counsel obedience on the picket lines and compliance with the system of labor control, in the Staley and Hormel disputes, workers broke through the barrier of compliance with the law, even if many of their actions were merely symbolic.

As well intentioned as they may be, though, symbolic actions, while they may gain media attention, still allow production to continue. As Peter Rachleff explained in summing up the use of civil disobedience during the Hormel strike, most strikers "admitted that they waited until it was too late to have an impact on the outcome of the struggle. For them it was more of an expression of moral witness than a tactic geared to effectively resisting employers and the government."[18] Steven Ashby and C.J. Hawking, in *Staley: The Fight For A New American Labor Movement*, drew similar conclusion from the Staley lockout, determining that "the corporate campaign alone was not enough to force the company to negotiate a fair contract. To be most effective, a corporate campaign should be combined with a strategy to stop or hinder production."[19]

It was Richard Trumka, leader of the successful Pittston strike, who clarified the difference between moral witness and what is actually takes to impact the production of an employer: "It has to be an ongoing effort that never ceases....You can't do it one day and then walk away for six months and do it again. It has to be an integral part of your strategy."[20] While the acts of civil disobedience in the Staley and Hormel struggles succeeded in garnering publicity, they differed fundamentally from the actions that traditional trade unionists of the 1930s engaged in. Traditional strike tactics were not about symbolism, but about stopping production. There is a reason that the critical labor battles of the 1930s have names such as the Battle of the Running Bulls or the Battle of Deputies Run. They were in fact fierce battles in which strikers saw defending their picket lines as the key to success. Even during sit-down strikes, workers prepared to defend the plant from police attack with water hoses and giant slingshots. While labor usually did not throw the first punch in these disputes, it was more than willing to fight back against employer goons or strikebreaking police. Unlike, for the most part, the labor movement of today.

HERE AND THE ATTEMPTS TO REBUILD AN INDUSTRY-WIDE APPROACH

As we have seen, one of the most effective tactics employers have used over the past several decades to diminish the labor movement is to eliminate the once dominant industry-wide approach to collective bargaining in favor of negotiating with individual unions one at a time. Disdained by the traditional labor movement, single union bargaining has allowing employers to use one union to undercut another, depressing wages, standards and organizing throughout a given industry.

One contemporary group that stands out in its attempt to revive an industry-wide approach to bargaining against large corporations is UNITE-HERE, the union of hotel workers. The group has adopted a long-term campaign called "Hotel Workers Rising" to unify dispersed local unions to take on giant national hotel chains. As John Wilhelm, the President of UNITE-HERE, explains, "We've become a globalized industry, so the old approach of our union in each city, standing on its own, didn't work anymore, and people were having increasing trouble bargaining and increasing trouble organizing."[21] Legal historian Julius Getman includes a detailed account of the UNITE-HERE campaign in his recent book *Restoring the Power of Unions: It Takes a Movement*. According to Getman, UNITE-HERE's approach is one of "member centered unionism."[22] Unlike SEIU, which created an industry-wide approach through the trampling of union democracy, labor management collaboration, and trusteeships, UNITE-HERE functions through sustained, member-driven activism.

UNITE-HERE has spent much of the last decade attempting to sync contract expiration dates in the hotel industry. During negotiations in Los Angeles and San Francisco in 2004, UNITE-HERE pushed for two-year contracts that would expire in 2006, the same year as contracts in other major cities such as Chicago, New York and Boston. In San Francisco, the hotel companies refused to agree on a two-year contract with the local union, who then launched a two-week strike at four hotels. The hotel companies retaliated with a lockout at fourteen hotels. However, with constant picket lines "turning away business, intense pressure from the San Francisco community, and solidarity actions throughout North America and the world, the hotels end their lockout in late November."[23] The members of the local then worked without a contract for two years until they were able to match their expiration date with the other cities in 2006. As of 2010, the UNITE-HERE campaign continues in full force. On July 22, 2010, thousands of UNITE-HERE members and supporters demonstrated against the Hyatt hotel chain in fifteen cities across the U.S. and Canada, with hundreds arrested for civil disobedience.[24]

The UNITE HERE example shows how a relatively decentralized union can push for coordinated bargaining rights without destroying local power. The test for UNITE-HERE will be whether they ultimately have the ability to economically harm employers. Even though they are bargaining on a coordinated basis nationally, the union cannot conduct a traditional strike without risking permanent replacement.

THREADS OF HISTORY

In August 2010, along with other trade unionists from the Twin Cities, I traveled ninety miles south to Austin, Minnesota to attend the 25th anniversary celebration of the Local P9 strike. To some the word "celebration" may seem misplaced, since the immediate result of that strike was a triumph for management.

However, to the P9 veterans in the room, many wearing their old "P9 Proud" union buttons, the word defeat does not remotely describe their feelings about the strike. Instead, as one now-elderly former striker said, "we were not defeated, since we never voted for that contract."

In the end, the greatest lesson trade unionists can draw from the labor struggles of the past few decades like P9 and Hormel and Pittston Coal and Staley and Republic Windows and the Charleston Five is simple and straightforward: don't be afraid to fight. Despite often being on the losing end of the conflict, these trade unionists maintained a militant tenacity, even in the face of extreme resistance from management, the government, even their own international union. Historically, this tenacity has been a hallmark of the labor movement, as socialist leader Eugene Debs once described so eloquently:

> "Ten thousand times has the labor movement stumbled and fallen and bruised itself, and risen again; been seized by the throat and choked and clubbed into insensibility; enjoined by courts, assaulted by thugs, charged by the militia, ... but, notwithstanding all this, and all these, it is today the most vital and potential power this planet has ever known...."[25]

Victory has never been a certainty for the labor movement; in fact, most of the time, the opposite has been true. But, despite often immense challenges, at times as grave as the loss of their lives, working people still banded together and fought for what was right, eventually establishing unions and creating a better life for generations of Americans during the twentieth century. Now that we are all well into the twenty-first century, the key question for trade unionists is can the labor movement once again become "the most vital and potential power this planet has ever known?"

9. WHERE DO WE GO FROM HERE?

After watching the labor movement—and the strike—wither over the past thirty years, trade unionists today need to answer several big questions if they wish to revitalize unions in this country. How should the labor movement deal with the current system of labor control? How should human labor be treated in relationship to capital? How can workers act as a class to advance their common interests? What are the best forms of organization to carry on the fight for workers' rights? And finally, what is the role of the strike? The answers—or non-answers—to these fundamental questions will shape labor's future in America.

As has been shown throughout this book, there are several fundamental propositions that, taken together, demonstrate that the current labor system is irretrievably broken. These include the following:

- Collective bargaining cannot work without an effective strike
- The system of labor control forbids effective strike tactics, including stopping production and workplace-based solidarity
- The various alternatives for union renewal (organizing without a strong strike, social unionism, corporate cam-

paigns, etc.) cannot revive the labor movement
- The labor movement has adopted a management-oriented way of thinking

The realization, in and of itself, that the system is not working actually represents the first step toward eventual trade union renewal. If trade unionists can admit that the system is broken, it then frees them to fashion a new form of unionism built around a revival of traditional tactics, including the effective strike.

A key task, then, is creating a broad-based understanding within the labor movement that things are fundamentally wrong. For many in the movement, who have become accustomed over the past three decades to taking two steps back for every step forward, this change in attitude will be difficult. However, it is a necessary step if there is going to be any possibility of reviving the labor movement as a viable force.

Trade unionism is, by its very nature, a narrow pursuit. Most trade unionists spend their days dealing with the little picture: the grievance of a fired co-worker, rating an organizing campaign, the drafting of proposals and counterproposals. These are not the sort of activities that encourage big ideas or broad thinking. This is not to say that the day-to-day struggles are not important, but keeping one's head down and simply fighting local battles is not the path to trade union renewal. As a trade unionist once told me, "I woke up one morning and realized I was dedicating my life to the more equitable distribution of overtime." This "small ball" approach has to change.

Unfortunately, for many trade unionists, the gulf between where they are and where they need to be, between today's realities and tomorrow's possibilities, seems so vast that a kind of intellectual paralysis sets in. Instead of envisioning a new, powerful labor movement, they are content to muddle along, fighting grievances, negotiating contracts, running union reform campaigns, spending their entire careers entrenched in what is at its core a fundamentally unjust system. Historically, the labor movement was about so much more than that. It was about inspiration and struggle, about ordinary people transforming the world—and themselves in the process. After three decades of defeat and decline, it is hard for many contemporary trade unionists to imagine a world in which the labor movement wields any real power.

Even if the labor movement is able to take that first step and admit that things cannot continue as they are, fixing the movement will be no easy task, as the current system of labor control is extremely well entrenched. Structurally, union density is at an all-time low in many industries, while, philosophically, the labor movement, including its progressive wing, remains mired in limited, conservative thinking. The factors that had underlain union strength in the 1930s, such as a powerful left and urban density, no longer exist.

However, great obstacles can potentially yield significant benefits. In the case of the labor movement, three decades' worth of failed policies has left an obvious opening for new, radical approaches. As a number of commentators have suggested, it is time for the labor movement to ask itself whether the current system is so irretrievably broken that it might not be better to try and establish entirely new versions of trade unionism. As SEIU staffer Steven Lerner argues, "If we don't seize the opportunity of the current economic crisis to chart a radically different course—committing ourselves and our movement to organizing for transformative change—we will sink into a deserved abyss of irrelevance."[1]

Presently, the majority of trade unionists do not participate in the debate over the future of the labor movement. In part, this is because the top down nature of most unions does not welcome or even permit debate. From tightly-controlled conventions to a union press lacking the freedom to question the prevailing wisdom, current union structures are set up to avoid honest discussion. Currently, the "debate", if one can call it that, over labor's future is mainly confined to academic journals and progressive union staffers. In "Reading, Writing and Union Building," Steve Early recounts the difficulties in even getting labor books in the hands of working class readers. Despite fifteen million members of organized labor, selling a mere 5,000 copies of a labor book is considered a runaway success.[2]

What then can be done to restart the struggle? One of the simplest steps is to help spread the debate. For example, set up a book club in your town, and discuss the ideas in this book, or any labor book. By performing this basic act, you can begin to put trade union theory back into the hands of the working class. Another idea is to sponsor a local speakers' club to discuss labor issues. During the 1990s, activists in the Twin Cities sponsored the Labor Speakers Club, which hosted speakers and discussions on a monthly basis. Also in the Twin Cities, a mixture of local labor activists and union officers (this author included) formed the Meeting the Challenge Committee, which held annual conferences that discussed the big questions facing the labor movement. Such efforts involved local trade union activists in the debate over labor's future.

BUILDING A TREND WITHIN THE LABOR MOVEMENT

To point the labor movement in a new direction will require more than fostering discussion, however; it will require a large group of people willing to challenge the status quo, people who have the ideas, organizational skills and self-confidence to give voice to a workers' movement capable of transforming America. This will have to start with the activists in the movement—shop floor militants, progressive union staffers and officers, worker centers' activists, and friendly academics. However, the debate over the future of trade unionism must grow beyond this committed, but small group if the there is to be a true labor revival in this country.

So how does one build such a trend? Again, we can learn from labor history. In the 1920s and early 1930s, the labor movement was stuck in a narrow form of craft unionism that was unable to win gains from employers. Craft unionists viewed only skilled workers as deserving of union representation, and they rejected attempts to organize all workers into one union. However, a countercurrent developed which argued that industrial unionism was the road forward for the labor movement. This trend toward industrial unionism was driven by the political left of the era (socialists, anarchists, and communists), who had a program that, although varying in its approaches, shared one guiding principle: the strength of the overall trade union movement.

This trend toward industrial unionism did not spring out of thin air, however, as these left wing groups had spent the first several decades of the twentieth century agitating—both inside and outside of the labor movement—for their aims. On the outside, the Industrial Workers of the World had strongly supported industrial unionism in both deed and action, while within the AFL, William Z. Foster and John Kirkpatrick of the Chicago Federation of Labor had organized the great 1919 nationwide steel strike. No matter the battle or the union, the idea behind it was always the same for these industrial trade unionists—one employer, one union.

Eventually, the years of agitation paid off as the idea of industrial unionism gained popularity, first at a grassroots level, and then broadly within the entire working class. Thus, when the economic crisis of the 1930s hit, workers were ready to embrace a new form of unionism. In *Heroes of Unwritten Story*, Henry Kraus, the editor of an early autoworkers' newsletter, recounts how workers in the 1930s rejected the narrow AFL craft unionism and fought to establish industrial organization. Kraus talks about how he was sitting in a local autoworker's union office shortly after the great sit-down strike at General Motors when a delegation of six workers from a sausage pickling plant came in. After determining where they worked, Kraus tried to direct the workers to an AFL craft union. Despite the fact that 500 of their fellow workers were sitting down at the plant to demand union recognition, these workers vehemently rejected the AFL, snarling "we don't want no truck with the AFL."[3] The task today is to build such a broad-based understanding within the labor movement of the need to change the present system.

How can this be done? During the decades-long push to establish industrial unionism in the first half of the twentieth century, industrial union activists repeatedly raised their issues at union conventions. Following their historical lead, trade unionists today could adopt the position that the system of labor control is illegitimate, and support efforts to break free from it. This could take the form of convention resolutions as a way of raising the debate within the movement. Just as it was once official AFL policy to disobey injunctions, trade unionists today could debate whether or not to comply with the different facets of the system of labor control.

No matter the issues, reviving the strike—and by extension, the labor movement—will require a single-minded focus by trade unionists. Right now, the left wing of the labor movement lacks a common agenda, as it advances a hodge-podge of ideas of what it will take to save unionism in this country. If one agrees with the analysis in this book, then the one unifying factor that can achieve the myriad goals of the labor movement is the revival of the effective, production-halting strike. This must become labor's primary focus.

Additionally, if trade unionists ever decide to embrace a new militancy in order to smash the system of labor control, they will need the support of their union brothers and sisters. Historian Nelson Lichtenstein, in the conclusion of his influential history of the labor movement, State of the Union, lists the failure to support militancy as one of the major weaknesses of the modern labor movement. Discussing what the movement needs to succeed, Lichtenstein noted,

> The first is militancy. The union movement needs more of it, but even more important, American labor as a whole needs to stand behind those exemplary instances of class combat when and if they occur. The 1980s where a tragic decade for unions, not because workers did not fight, but where labor did take a stand—at International Paper in Jay, Maine; at Phelps Dodge in Arizona; at Hormel in Austin, Minnesota; at Continental and Greyhound— their struggles were both physically isolated and ideologically devalued.[4]

Instead of being engulfed in the solidarity of their fellow trade unionists, workers today who chose to fight back often do so on lonely picket lines, with little support from the official labor movement. Without a broad trend that promotes effective tactics, striking workers are not exposed to ideas that can help them win strikes, nor are they supported when they engage in militancy.

In the past, even during labor's darkest hours, workers were able to reach deep down to create new methods of struggle that transformed the political landscape, methods that relied on worker militancy and solidarity, supported by an effective strike. While the strike might seem like a relic of the past to much of the contemporary labor movement, as labor historian Peter Rachleff writes, "it would be a mistake to leap to the conclusion that strikes are on their way to the dustbin of history. As long as the capitalist economy rests on the employment and exploitation of labor, the organized withdrawal of labor is bound to remain a central expression of working class protest and power."[5]

CREATING NEW UNIONS TO PROTECT OLD UNIONS

Because of the legal shackles placed on unions by nearly seventy-five years' worth of anti-worker judicial decisions, it is nearly impossible for trade unions as currently constituted to escape the system of labor control. Therefore, reviving trade unionism will require creating new organizations that are willing and able to take the risks associated with violating labor law, which is the only means available to trade unionists who want to engage in an effective strike.

One legal constraint that has done much to tame the labor movement is a little known provision of the Taft-Hartley Act that authorizes lawsuits against unions for damages, including violations of secondary boycott provisions.[6] According to Section 301 of the Act, a union "shall be bound by the acts of its agents. Any such labor organization may sue or be sued as an entity."[7] Thus, any union that violates a no strike clause, defies a court order, or violates the Taft Hartley restrictions on secondary strikes faces employer damage suits and fines by the courts. This provision was designed specifically to stop union militancy; by threatening unions with the possibility of a large hit to their pocketbooks, employers and courts have been able to pressure union officials to keep their own members in line.

During the strike at Pittston Coal in 1989, the United Mineworkers of America were assessed $64 million in fines.[8] Even after the conclusion of the strike, the judge refused to vacate most of the fines. The case eventually went to the Supreme Court, which determined that the judge had not followed proper procedure in imposing the fines. As Eddie Burke, one of the leaders of the strike, once said, "Lawyers will always give you arguments why you shouldn't do something. We faced fines of $500,000 a day before we sat down in the mines. But we did what we had to do."[9] The UMWA, with its tradition of militancy and reform leadership, was willing to take a financial risk in the name of principle.

Unfortunately, few contemporary unions are willing to take the kind of risks that the UMWA did during the Pittston strike. Today's international unions are large organizations with hundreds of employees and hundreds of millions of dollars in assets, all of which are subject to attachment in damage suits in the event of a strike. Therefore, protecting these assets is a primary goal of these unions. While this may be a legitimate concern, as Steven Lerner of the SEIU remarked, "if we continue the way we are going, we may save buildings and investments but our ability to fulfill our mission of organizing, representing workers, and improving society is zero. Big treasuries don't help if we have no members."[10]

To help unions protect their financial assets in the event of a strike, in 2005, the American Federation of Teachers proposed that, when organizing in new industries, unions establish independent organizations that would not be subject to lawsuits by employers. This type of organizing would "require creating new unions from scratch and even adopting unconventional tactics unencumbered by the restraints of current labor law." Understanding that unions have much to "risk and lose through the purposeful violation of Taft-Hartley," the proposal stated that these so-called "start-up unions," possessing no financial assets, "might enjoy greater strategic and tactical flexibility and would have substantially less to lose through the smart and strategic use of unconventional approaches where appropriate."[11]

While companies have long engaged in these types of legal maneuvers, such as the transfer of work to allegedly separate, non-union subsidiaries to avoid unionization, or reopening under "new" ownership to divest itself of the union, unions have failed to use these same kinds of maneuvers for their own purposes. However, with no assets or buildings to seize, both the government and employers would have no financial threat over the types of organizations advocated for in the AFT proposal.

There is a historical precedent for such new forms of organization. In the 1930s, with the debate raging over industrial unionism, the AFL directly chartered federal locals. These locals organized workers, with the idea that which unions the workers belonged to would be sorted out later on. In another example from the 1930s, John L. Lewis and the United Mine Workers of America determined that to secure bargaining rights for mineworkers, workers in other basic industries also had to be organized. To make this happen, the UMWA put up millions of dollars to fund the unionization drive of the United Autoworkers and the Steelworkers. While the Mineworkers did not gain dues from the organizing drive, they understood that the only way to achieve their bargaining goals was to organize other basic industries.

Although independent, it would still be important that such organizations have the support of the existing labor movement. Otherwise, they will be isolated politically, vulnerable to attack by employers and the government. Absent union support, such organizations would also be subject to the charge of dual unionism. In the past, when workers formed independent, militant unions, the AFL-CIO would accuse them of forming dual unions and undermining the labor movement. Back when unions had jurisdictions over industries and established union patterns, there were economic reasons for the hostility to dual unions. Today, however, with the decline in patterns and the move towards general unionism, those concerns have lost much of their validity.

While some international unions might feel threatened by the kind of independent organizations advocated by the AFT, building a militant pole within the labor movement would help all unions grow by allowing them to engage in new, bold tactics. For example, in the 1930s, the explosion of the militant CIO unions prompted major growth even for the more conservative AFL unions. If international unions ultimately choose not to fund such independent organizations on a major scale, local unions and progressive unionists could step in and sponsor them instead.

Though the AFT proposal would regard these newly created unions mainly as tools for organizing new industries, there is no reason that these organizations could not be used to bargain existing contracts. For example, if a union were facing a tough strike, bargaining rights could be transferred to an independent organization. Strike funds could then be placed in a trust, and formal ties to the union would be cut.

In trying to develop new forms of organization, labor can learn much from the worker center movement. Worker centers, which are community-based organizations that address workplace issues for a particular community of workers, came to the forefront in the 1990s. As of 2005, there were 137 workers centers in the United States, 122 of them based in immigrant communities.[12] These centers provide organization for the most exploited sections of the working class, including day laborers, domestic workers, and farm workers.

Worker centers possess several strengths, in particular, the ability to organize sections of the working class not usually reachable by unions. Worker centers are also able to draw in workers across employers and industries to fight for common concerns. Using grassroots activism, they pressure employers through picketing, lawsuits, and other methods. Not tied into the narrow bargaining structure fostered by the NLRA, they are free to push for solutions that cut across employers, such as demanding that all employers at a shopping mall pay a living wage.

Despite all the good that they do, worker centers have some fundamental weaknesses that limit their ability to play a larger role in the revival of the labor movement. The first is a lack of independent funding. According to Janice Fine, a professor of Labor Relations at Rutgers University, while some worker centers attempt to collect membership dues, these monies only account for two percent of their funding. A majority of the funding—61 percent—comes from foundations, while the government chips in 21 percent, with the remaining sixteen percent coming from earned income and grassroots fundraising.[13] If worker centers ever became a vehicle for more militant action, their foundation funding would likely evaporate.

More importantly, however, is that, like the rest of the labor movement, worker centers are stuck within the system of labor control. To truly raise wage rates of the low income workers they represent, worker centers would need to engage in the militant tactics of workplace based solidarity and stopping production. Like unions, breaking free from the constraints imposed by labor law would be necessary if worker centers are to play a larger role in revitalizing the labor movement, a scenario that, at present, seems unlikely. Still, it is possible that some characteristics of worker centers—in particular, their ability to reach groups of workers that unions currently are unable to—could be utilized by a new, fighting labor movement.

REVIVING SOLIDARITY

According to author Dan Clawson, if there is to be union growth in the future, it will likely come as part of a wave of organizing during a social upsurge.[14] There is historical precedent for this, in both the private and public sector. In the private sector, unionism exploded during the CIO march to organize basic industries, such as auto and steel, in the 1930s, while during the 1960s, the civil rights and other social movements produced massive gains in public sector union membership. Unions did not expand one shop at a time during these surges, but rather ballooned up in large bursts mainly as the result of ordinary working people taking it upon themselves to organize and fight for change.

However, today's the system of labor control is structured to prevent such an upsurge. Instead of collective action, the present system fosters individualism, as employers seek to narrow the scope of labor disputes by focusing on the so-called "rights" of workers. The reason that employer funded anti-union organizations have names such as the National Right to Work Foundation is so they can pose as the guardians of worker rights while, in reality, they are eviscerating those rights. Anti-labor conservatives have learned that it benefits the cause of employers to frame the discussion in terms of individual rights: the "right" of a scab to cross a picket line, the "right" of a worker to not to join a union, the "right" of an employer to denigrate unions to a captive audience of workers. The underlying philosophy behind this worker's "rights" rhetoric is the narrowing of disputes in the workplace to employees and their immediate employer.

To break out of this rhetorical straightjacket, unions must move past the emphasis on the individual rights of workers—which is really just a backhanded way of keeping workers down—to rediscovering a solidarity that focuses on the greater good of all employees. The labor movement has plenty of slogans that speak to the importance of worker solidarity: "an injury to one is an injury to all," "El pueblo unido jamas sera vencido," "solidarity forever," and "you can hang together or you can hang alone." It is time to start adapting these slogans to real world action.

Reviving solidarity in this way will require new approaches to unionism based not on workers focusing on narrow battles with individual employers but, rather, on fighting for larger issues and causes. As an example, arguably the most important strike of the last decade was conducted not by trade unionists over a labor dispute, but by immigrant workers and supporters angry over a political decision, when, on May Day, 2006, millions of protesters gathered in cities across the U.S. to protest the government's new, tougher immigration policy. The theme of the protests was a "Day Without Immigrants," a takeoff on the popular film, A Day Without Mexicans. Though not specifically over a labor issue, the strike nevertheless impacted production nationwide in industries that employed Latino labor. A *New York Times* article the day after the protests described their affect:

> Lettuce, tomatoes and grapes went unpicked in fields in California and Arizona, which contribute more than half the nation's produce, as scores of growers let workers take the day off. Truckers who move 70 percent of the goods in ports in Los Angeles and Long Beach, Calif., did not work. Meatpacking companies, including Tyson Foods and Cargill, closed plants in the Midwest and the West employing more than 20,000 people, while the flower and produce markets in downtown Los Angeles stood largely and eerily empty.[15]

In other countries around the world, notably France, workers respond to attempts to eliminate social programs not through letter or email campaigns to politicians, but through direct action involving millions of workers. However, in the United States, such efforts have been restricted by the system of labor control. This is why the immigrant workers' strike was so significant.

Ultimately, if the end goal is to create industry-wide solutions to the problems that the labor movement faces, this idea must be reflected in trade union strategy from the get-go. Currently, entire industries of the private sector are essentially unorganized, including trucking, financial and retail. Reorganizing these industries will not happen on a shop-by-shop basis, so trade unionists need to quit trying to organize in this manner and focus instead on rebuilding worker solidarity.

In the 1930s, trade unionists determined what forms of

union struggle would improve workers' lives, and then embraced these forms, whatever the risks. For example, understanding that they could easily be replaced by scabs in the event of a strike, traditional trade unionists engaged in the sit-down strike. Realizing that organizing thousands of small trucking companies one by one would not work, trade unionists instead piggybacked off union strength through solidarity tactics. The first and foremost consideration in all these efforts was whether such tactics could work.

If today's labor movement adopted such an approach, seasoned activists could examine the weaknesses of employers in various industries and devise strategies to exploit these weaknesses. In trucking for example, it is hard to see how unions could reorganize the industry employer by employer, as the competitive pressures on any single unionized employer would be too great. However, an approach based not on traditional unionism, but on creating a nationwide truckers organization agitating for improved standards for truckers, and striking if necessary to back up those demands, would at least have the potential for success.

Ultimately, trade unionists must ask some hard questions: If workers are choosing not to join unions, then what forms of organization do they want to create instead? If organizing shop-by-shop cannot work, what approach can? And, if conventional approaches to unionization are not succeeding, which ones can?

LABOR'S FUTURE

In the first months of 2011, anti-labor conservatives launched a coordinated offensive against the last remaining stronghold of unionization, the public sector. In state after state, Republican-dominated legislatures introduced legislation to restrict the ability of public sector unions to collectively bargain. Not content with driving unionization down to levels not seen since the early 1900s, these conservatives dream of a United States with no unions whatsoever, in which the power of capital reigns supreme. Abhorring the very idea of a public sphere, they seek to privatize public education, gut health and safety laws, and wipe out a century of progressive taxation. Already, with the far right in control of the Supreme Court, a century old limitation on direct corporate contributions to political campaigns has been overturned. As progressive commentator Chris Hedges notes in the *Death of the Liberal Class*, the institutions of mainstream liberalism cannot and will not confront this corporate power.[16] That is why the revival of the labor movement is about more than just the fate of the strike—at stake is the right's ability to transform American culture in its own image.

In February and March of 2011, tens of thousands of workers and supporters took to the streets of Madison, Wisconsin to defend not only their unions, but the very idea of collective bargaining. Responding to Governor Scott Walker's attempt to strip public employees in the state of their bargaining rights, workers and ordinary citizens surrounded the state capitol, while thousands of teachers called in sick, understanding that caring for their students meant defending their profession. Eventually, students and workers occupied the capitol building for weeks, shaking the corridors of power with their signature chant, "This is What Democracy Looks Like." Instead of the sterile pre-printed signs favored by many unions, protestors showed up with carefully crafted homemade signs. Private sector workers, resisting the divisive arguments of conservative commentators, joined with their public sector sisters and brothers to defend collective bargaining.

Through a great grassroots struggle, reminiscent of the heyday of the traditional labor movement, workers in Wisconsin altered the terms of the debate from one of greedy trade unionists to the broader notions of the right to bargain and corporate control of the economy. Poll after poll demonstrated that trade unionists won this debate, with the public decisively rejecting Governor Walker's proposed legislation. In terms of the duration of the struggle, the intensity of the response, and the sheer size of the demonstrations, what happened in Wisconsin was unlike any labor uprising in decades. Reflecting on this solidarity reveals the choice that the labor movement currently faces: to embrace and build upon the spirit and vitality displayed in Wisconsin, or continue with the failed strategies of the past thirty years, until trade unionism in this country is dead. For all those who believe in a better world, where working people are treated with respect and dignity, the choice is clear.

ACKNOWLEDGMENTS

As a college student in the mid-1980s, I traveled to Austin, Minnesota to join a picket-line with striking meatpackers at Hormel. Growing up in a union household, I was familiar with trade unionism, but supporting the striking members of Local P9 was my first exposure to intense labor conflict. Later, as a local union president and hospital worker in the early 1990s, I helped to build a fighting local at the University of Minnesota Medical Center. Our local also supported many of the other labor struggles of the time, including Staley, the Detroit News, and Pittston. From all these striking workers, I learned about solidarity and struggle, the limitations of corporate campaigns, the weakness of the modern strike, and the stranglehold of the system of labor control.

I first considered writing a book while at NYU Law School in the late 1990s. Reading works such as James Atleson's *Values and Assumptions in American Labor Law* and George Feldman's "Unions, Solidarity, and Class: The Limits of Liberal Labor Law" contributed greatly to my understanding of the system of labor control. By the time I got around to writing this book, I had spent a decade bargaining contracts in the healthcare and airline industries.

In the writing of this book, I have had the support and encouragement of many people. Kathy Kleckner put in countless hours providing input on content. Dick Taylor, a retired teacher, spent untold hours helping to refine the writing in the early stages of the manuscript. My brother and friend Jim Burns provided encouragement, while J Berger, Cherrene Horazuk, Joe Iosbaker, and Phyllis Walker, long-time friends and union activists, read through several drafts, providing invaluable feedback.

Steve Early, author of *The Civil Wars in US Labor*, provided contacts and tips on how to navigate the world of publishing. Labor historian Peter Rachleff offered helpful advice and suggestions throughout the writing process. *Labor Notes* journalist Jane Slaughter read an early draft of the manuscript, challenging some of my assertions. Robert Lasner and Elizabeth Clementson of Ig Publishing took a chance on a first-time author with a controversial topic. Robert's skillful editing vastly improved the final work. Finally, while researching the book, one scholar's work kept popping up. Whether the topic was restrictions on the sit-down strike or the radical underpinnings of traditional labor thought, I kept running into the the works of James Pope, who read an early draft of the book.

The labor movement can and will recover again in the United States. One may ask, what in these bleak times is the source of my optimism? It is two decades' worth of experience in the movement, seeing the willingness of working people to fight back, despite long odds. I have witnessed the determination and creativity shown by flight attendants in Milwaukee standing up to threats of termination to win a first contract, *Detroit News'* strikers taking on media giant Gannett, and nurses in Chicago joining with janitors to fight privatization. All these fights, and many, many others, give me hope for the future of the labor movement.

NOTES

1. THE STRIKE AND THE RISE OF THE WORKING CLASS

1. Albert Reese, *The Economics of Trade Unions* (Chicago: University of Chicago Press, 1962), 31.

2. Roy B. Helfgott, *Labor Economics* (New York: Random House, 1980), 172.

3. Jack Barbash, *The Practice of Unionism* (New York: Harper & Row, 1956), 213.

4. Bureau of Labor Statistics," "Work stoppages involving 1,000 or more workers, 1947-200," http://www.bls.gov/news.release/wkstp.t01. htm.

5. Sidney Fine, *Sit-down: the General Motors Strike of 1936-1937*, (Ann Arbor: University Press, 1969), 55-63.

6. Jack Metzgar, "The 1945-1946 Strike Wave" in *The Encyclopedia of Strikes in American History* edited by Aaron Brenner, Benjamin Day and Immanuel Ness (Armonk: M.E. Sharpe, 2009), 217.

7. Victor Reuther, *The Brothers Reuther and the Story of the UAW* (Boston: Houghton Mifflin, 1976), 310-11.

8. Jack Metzgar, *Striking Steel: Solidarity Remembered* (Philadelphia: Temple University Press, 2000), 36.

9. Metzgar, *Striking Steel,* 36.

10. Aaron Brenner, "Introduction" to the *Encyclopedia of Strikes in American History*, xxxi

11. Phillip S. Foner, *History of the Labor Movement in the United States: Volume 1 From Colonial Times to the Founding of the American Federation*

of Labor (International Publishers: New York, 1947).

12. Nelson Lichtenstein, S*tate of the Union: A Century of American Labor* (Princeton: Princeton University Press, 2002), 99.

13. Nelson Lichtenstein, *State of the Union*, 99.

14. Bureau of Labor Statistics, "Work stoppages involving 1,000 or more workers, 1947-2009," http://www.bls.gov/news.release/wkstp.t01.htm.

15. Joseph McCartin, "Approaching Extinction?: The Decline of Strikes in the United States, 1960-2005" in *Strikes Around the World, 1968-2005: Case Studies of 15 Countries* edited by Sjaak Van Der Velden, Heiner Dribbusch, and Dave Lyddon (Amsterdam: Aksant Academic Publishers, 2008), 141.

16. Kim Moody, *US Labor in Trouble and Transition* (London: Verso, 2007), 80.

17. Employee Benefits Research Institute, "Retirement Trends in the United States Over the Past Quarter-Century," http://www.ebri.org/pdf/publications/facts/0607fact.pdf.

18. Moody, *US Labor in Trouble and Transition*, 35.

19. John Logan, "Permanent Replacements and the End of Labor's 'Only True Weapon'," *International Labor and Working Class History* 74 (2008): 171.

20. Reynolds, *Power and Privilege: Labor Unions in America* (New York: Universe Books, 1984), 48.

21. Reynolds, *Power and Privilege*, 53.

22. Fine, *Sit-down: the General Motors Strike of 1936-1937*, 174.

23. Helfgott, *Labor Economics*, 173.

24. James Begin and Edwin Beal, *The Practice of Collective Bargaining* (Homewood: Richard D. Irwin, Inc., 1985), 228.

25. Begin, *The Practice of Collective Bargaining*, 232.

26. Bruce E. Kaufman, "Historical Insights: The Early Institutionalists on Trade Unionism and Labor Policy," in *What Do Unions Do: A Twenty Year Perspective edited by Bennett, James and Bruce Kaufman* (New Brunswick: Transaction Publishers, 2008), 61.

27. Philip Taft, *Organized Labor in American History* (New York: Harper & Row, 1964), 183.

28. John Commons, *History of Labour in the United States, Volume II*

(New York: MacMillan, 1918), 43.

29. Commons, *History of Labour Volume II*, 44.

30. Lloyd Ulman, *The Rise of the National Trade Union* (Cambridge: Harvard University Press, 1955).

31. John Schmitt and Kris Warner, "The Changing Face of Labor, 1983-2008," Center for Economic and Policy Research, http://www.cepr.net/documents/publications/changing-face-of-labor-2009-11.pdf.

32. The Pew Research Center for the People & the Press, "Favorability Ratings of Labor Unions Fall Sharply," http://people-press.org/report/591/.

2. THE TURBULENT 1930S

1. Charles Craypo, *The Economics of Collective Bargaining: Case Studies in the Private Sector* (Washington, D.C.: BNA Books, 1986), 226.

2. See Mark Linder, *Wars of Attrition: Vietnam, the Business Roundtable, and the Decline of Construction Unions* (Iowa City: Fanpihua Press, 1999) for a full analysis of building trades power.

3. For a good account of the battle to control the hiring of unions see WilliamMillikan, *Union Against Unions: The Minneapolis Citizens Alliance and Its Fights Against Organized Labor, 1903-1947* (St Paul: Minnesota Historical Society Press, 2003).

4. Philip Taft and Philip Ross, "American Labor Violence: Its Causes, Character and Outcome" in H.D. Graham and T.R. Gurr, eds., *The History of Violence in America: Historical and Comparative Perspectives* (New York: Praeger, 1969), 281.

5. Jeremy Brecher, *Strike!* (Greenwich: Fawcett Premier, 1974), 81-93.

6. Theresa Ann Case, "Labor Upheaval on the Nation's Railroads, 1877-1922 in Brenner, *Encyclopedia of Strikes*, 2009.

7. Norwood, *Strike Breaking and Intimidation: Mercenaries and Masculinity in Twentieth-Century America* (Chapel Hill: University of North Carolina Press), 34.

8. James Robinson and Roger Walker, *Labor Economics and Labor Relations* (New York: Ronald Press Co., 1973), 172-173.

9. Bernstein, *The Turbulent Years: A History of the American Worker,*

1933-1940 (Chicago: Haymarket Books), 217-317.

10. Brecher, *Strike!*, 200-202; Bernstein, *The Turbulent Years*, 222-224.

11. Janet Irons, *Testing the New Deal, The General Textile Strike of 1934 in the American South* (Urbana: University of Illinois Press, 2000), 129.

12. Brecher, *Strike!*, 204; Bernstein, *The Turbulent Years*, 235.

13. Bernstein, *The Turbulent Years*, 238.

14. Brecher, *Strike!*, 211.

15. Barbash, *The Practice of Unionism*, 232.

16. Bernstein, *The Turbulent Years*, 500.

17. Fine, *Sit-down*, 123-125.

18. Fine, *Sit-down*, 172.

19. Vivian M. Baulch and Patricia Zacharias, "The Historic 1936-37 Flint Auto Plant Strikes," *Detroit News*, June 23, 1197, http://apps.detnews.com/apps/history/index.php?id=115

20. Although, as James Pope notes, labor advanced varying justifications for the right to strike. James Gray Pope, "The Thirteenth Amendment versus the Commerce Clause: Labor and the Shaping of American Constitutional Law, 1921-1957," *Columbia Law Review* 102 (January 2002).

21. Drew D. Hansen, "The Sit-Down Strikes and the Switch in Time," *Wayne Law Review* 46 (Spring 2000).

22. Rachel Mayer, "The Rise and Fall of the Sit-down Strike" in *The Encyclopedia of Strikes*, 210.

23. Jane Slaughter, "Corporate Campaigns: Labor Enlists Community Support" in *Building Bridges: The Emerging Grassroots Coalition of Labor and Community*, edited by Jeremy Brecher and Tim Costello (New York: Monthly Review Press, 1990), 49.

24. Donald Garnel, *The Rise of Teamster Power in the West* (Berkeley: University of California Press, 1972), 115. See also Dobbs, Farrel, *Teamster Power* (New York: Pathfinder Press 1973) for the pioneering work of left wing Minneapolis Teamsters in utilizing secondary activity to organize truckers throughout the Midwest in the 1930s.

25. Garnel, *The Rise of Teamster Power in the West*, 112.

26. Garnel, *The Rise of Teamster Power*, 114.

27. William Forbath, *Law and the Shaping of the American Labor Movement* (Cambridge: Harvard University Press, 1991), 83.

28. Phillip Foner, *History of the Labor Movement in the United States, Volume II* (New York, International Publishers, 1955), 48.

29. Foner, *History of the Labor Movement in the United States, Volume II*, 48.

30. Henry Laidler, *Boycotts and the Labor Struggle: Economic and Legal Aspects* (New York: John Lane Company, 1913).

31. William Millikan, *A Union against Unions: The Minneapolis Citizens Alliance and Its Fight against Organized Labor, 1903–1947* (St. Paul: Minnesota Historical Society Press, 2001), 63.

32. Begin, *The Practice of Collective Bargaining*, 228.

3. THE OUTLAWING OF SOLIDARITY AND THE DECLINE OF THE STRIKE

1. Tomlins, *The State and the Unions: Labor Relations, Law, and the Organized Labor Movement in America, 1880-1960* (Cambridge: Cambridge University Press, 1985), 124-125.

2. David Brody, "Labor vs. The Law: How the Wagner Act Became a Management Tool," *New Labor Forum* 13 no. 1, (2004): 10.

3. Harry A. Millis and Emily Clark Brown, *From the Wagner Act to Taft-Hartley: A Study of National Labor Policy and Labor Relations* (Chicago: University of Chicago Press, 1950), 283.

4. Nelson Lichtenstein, "Taft-Hartley: A Slave-Labor Law?," *Catholic University Law Review* (Spring 1998): 767.

5. Lichtenstein, "Taft-Hartley: A Slave-Labor Law," 767.

6. Lichtenstein, "Taft-Hartley: A Slave-Labor Law," 765.

7. James Gray Pope, "The First Amendment, the Thirteenth Amendment, and the Right to Organize in the Twenty-First Century," *Rutgers Law Review* 51 (1999): 94. See also James Gray Pope, "Labor-Community Coalitions and Boycotts: The Old Labor Law, the New Unionism, and the Living Constitution," *Texas Law Review* 69 (1991): 889.

8. Tomlins, *The State and the Unions*, 251.

9. Daniels Cletus, *The ACLU and the Wagner Act: An Inquire into the Depression-Era Crisis of American Liberalism* (Ithaca: Cornel University,

1980), 102.

10. Lichtenstein, "Taft-Hartley: A Slave-Labor Law," 786.

11. Lichtenstein, "Taft-Hartley: A Slave-Labor Law," 787.

12. John Higgens, ed., *The Developing Labor Law, 5th Edition* (Washington, D.C.: BNA Books, 2006), 712-730.

13. Higgens, *The Developing Labor Law*, 853-854.

14. Moody, *An Injury to All*, 165 – 191.

15. Moody, *An Injury to All*, 182.

16. Moody, *An Injury to All*, 174.

17. Staughton Lynd, "Book Review: Ideology and Labor Law," *Stanford Law Review* 36 (1984): 1273-1284.

18. Staughton Lynd, ed., *American Labor Radicalism: Testimonies and Interpretations* (New York: John Wiley & Sons, 1973), 5.

19. *NLRB v. Sands Mfg. Co.*, 306 US 332 (1939). See Higgens, *The Developing Labor Law*, 1623-1625 for discussion of the intricacies of this area.

20. Higgens, *The Developing Labor Law*, 1447-1476.

21. Labor - 29 U.S.C.. § 101

22. See the *Developing Labor Law, Fourth Edition*, 498 et sequence.

23. *Gateway Coal v. Mine Workers District 4, Local 6330*, 414 US 368 (1974). See *Buffalo Forge v Steelworkers*, 428 US 397 (1976) stating that a sympathy strike during term of agreement not enjoinable.

24. George Feldman, "Unions, Solidarity, and Class: The Limits of Liberal Labor Law," *Berkeley Journal of Employment & Labor Law* 15 (1994): 187.

25. James Pope, "Worker Lawmaking, Sit-Down Strikes, and the Shaping of American Industrial Relations, 1935-1958," *Law & History Review* 24, no. 4 (2006): 61.

26. *NLRB v. Fansteel Metallurgical Corp*, 306 US 240 (1939).

27. James Pope, "How American Workers Lost the Right to Strike," *Michigan Law Review* 103(2004): 518, 521.

28. Higgens, *The Developing Labor Law*, 1606-1618.

29. Walter H. Uphoff, *Kohler on Strike: Thirty Years of Conflict* (Boston: Beacon Press, 1966). For a pro-employer account see Sylvester Petro, *Kohler Strike: Union Violence and Administrative Law* (Chicago: Henry

Regnery Co, 1961).

30. Wisconsin Historical Society, "Dictionary of Wisconsin History: Kohler Strike," http://www.wisconsinhistory.org/dictionary/index.asp?action=view&term_id=284&term_type_id=3&term_type_text=things&letter=K

31. Higgens, *The Developing Labor Law,* 2361 -2368.

32. "Nation: The Golden Handshake," *Time magazine,* December 24, 1965, http://www.time.com/time/magazine/article/0,9171,834841,00.html

33. John Logan, "Permanent Replacements and the End of Labor's 'Only True Weapon'," *International Labor and Working Class History* 74 (2008): 171.

34. Mathew Finkin, "Labor Policy and the Enervation of the Economic Strike," *University of Illinois Law Review,* 1990, 547-567.

35. Finkin, "The Enervation of the Economic Strike," 567.

36. Albert Rees, *Economics of Trade Unions,* 34-35.

37. James Gray Pope, "Essay: How American Workers Lost the Right to Strike, and Other Tales, *Michigan Law Review* 103 (2004):533-34.

38. Neil Chamberlain, *Collective Bargaining* (New York: McGraw-Hill, 1965), 400.

39. Michael H. LeRoy, "Regulating Employer Use of Permanent Striker Replacements: Empirical Analysis of NLRA and RLA Strikes 1935-1991," *Berkeley Journal of Employment and Labor Law* 16 (1995): 169.

40. Joseph A. McCartin, "'Fire the Hell Out of Them': Sanitation Workers' Struggles and the Normalization of the Striker Replacement Strategy in the 1970s," *Labor: Studies in the Working-Class History of the Americas* 2.3 (2005): 70.

41. Holly Knaus, "Labor's Lost Right to Strike" *Multinational Monitor,* July 1992, http://multinationalmonitor.org/hyper/issues/1992/07/mm0792_13.html

42. John Logan, "Permanent Replacements," 177. See also Mathew Finkin, "Labor Policy and the Enervation of the Economic Strike," 547.

43. Barbash, *The Practice of Unionism,* 227.

44. Kim Moody, *An Injury to All: The Decline of American Unionism* (London: Verso, 1988); Mike Davis *Prisoners of the American Dream*, (London: Verso, 1986).

45. Rosenblum, *Copper Crucible*, 217.

46. Higgens, *The Developing Labor Law*, 598-606.

47. Lance Compa, "Blood, Sweat and Fear: Workers Rights in US Meat and Poultry Plants," Human Rights Watch, 2004, http://www.hrw.org/reports/2005/usa0105/.

4. LABOR'S FAILED SEARCH FOR ALTERNATIVES TO THE STRIKE

1. For a good statement of the current law regarding these tactics see Robert M. Schwartz, *Strikes, Picketing and Inside Campaigns: A Legal Guide for Unions* (Cambridge: Work Rights Press, 2006).

2. Dan La Botz, "Strikes" in *Slaughter, Troublemakers Handbook II*, 109. While most union contracts no longer allow mid-contract strikes, the International Union of Electrical Workers contract with GE allowed strikes if the employer raised health care costs mid contract. The IUE struck to demonstrate resolve going into negotiations.

3. Federal Mediation and Conciliation Service, http://www.fmcs.gov/internet/downloadsList.asp?categoryID=276.

4. Aaron Brenner, "Inside Strategies" in *Slaughter, Troublemakers Handbook II*, 127.

5. Pam Galperin, "Telephone Workers Pressure Verizon from Within" in in *Slaughter, Troublemakers Handbook II*, 131-134.

6. Jane Slaughter, "Corporate Campaigns," 56.

7. Employers consistently assert the tactic is illegal and they will fire workers who engage in the tactic. See Borer, David and Joe Burns, "Flight Attendants Wreak Havoc" in *Slaughter, Troublemakers Handbook II*, 134.

8. Craig Becker, "Better Than a Strike: Protecting New Forms of Collective Work Stoppages under the National Labor Relations Act," *Univeristy of Chicago Law Review* 61 (1994): 351.

9. Craig Becker, "Better Than a Strike," 387.

10. Craig Becker, "Better Than a Strike," 388.

11. Amy Dean and David Reynolds, *How Regional Activism Will Re-*

shape the American Labor Movement (Ithaca: ILR Press, 2009).

12. Dan Clawson, *The Next Upsurge*, 16.

13. Fantasia, *Cultures of Solidarity,* 92.

14. Steven K. Ashby and C. J. Hawking, *The Fight for a New American Labor Movement* (University of Illinois Press, 2009), 218.

15. Rachleff, *Hard-Pressed in the Heartland*, 61.

16. These exceptions include: Mark Dudzic, "Saving the Right to Organize: Substituting the Thirteenth Amendment for the Wagner Act," *New Labor Forum* 14 (2005): 59-67; Micheal Eisenriecher, "Is the Secret to Labor's Future in Its Past?"; *WorkingUSA* 5 (2002):95-122; James Pope, Ed Bruno and Peter Kellman, "Towards A New Labor Rights Movement" *WorkingUSA* 4 (2001): 8-33; Peter Rachleff, "Is the Strike Dead?" *New Labor Forum* 12 (2003): 87-94.

17. Aaron Brenner, Robert Brenner, and Cal Winslow, *Rebel Rank and File: Labor Militancy and Revolt from Below During the Long 1970s* (New York: Verso, 2010).

18. Ray Tillman and Michael Cummings, *The Transformation of US Unions: Voices, Visions, and Strategies from the Grassroot*s (Boulder: Lynne Rienner, 1999), 272.

19. Fletcher, *Solidarity Divided,* 52.

20. Robert Fitch, "Card Check: Labor's Charlie Brown Moment?", *New Politics* 12, no. 4 (Winter 2010), http://newpolitics.mayfirst.org/fromthearchives?nid=178. See also Fitch, *Solidarity for Sale.*

21. Mike Parker and Martha Gruelle, *Democracy is Power: Rebuilding Unions from the Bottom Up* (Detroit: Labor Education and Research Project, 2005), 14.

5. WHY ORGANIZING CANNOT SOLVE THE LABOR CRISIS

1. Kim Moody, *US Labor in Trouble and Transition*, 100; "Union Membership and Coverage Database," http://www.unionstats.com/.

2. Kim Moody, *US Labor in Trouble and Transition*,128.

3. Steven Lerner, "An Immodest Proposal: A New Architecture For the House of Labor," *New Labor Forum* 12, no 2. (2003):16-17 .

4. Lerner, "An Immodest Proposal," 16.

5. Richard Hurd, "The Failure of Organizing, the New Unity Partner-

ship, and the Future of the Labor Movement," *WorkingUSA: The Journal of Labor and Society 8* (2004:) 5–25, 17.

6. Adrienne Eaton, Janice Fine, Allison Porter and Saul Rubinstein, "Organizational Change at SEIU: 1996—2009," March 2010, 14.

7. Service Employees International Union, www.seiu.org. SEIU's LM2 report filed with the department of labor shows 1,857,136 members in 2009, although that number does not necessarily include the 100,000 Canadian members.

8. Steve Early, *Embedded with Organized Labor: Journalistic Reflections on the Class War at Home* (New York: Monthly Review Press, 2009), 212.

9. Eaton, "Organizational Change at SEIU," 46.

10. Alec MacGillis, "At the Peak of his Influence, SEIU Chief Set to Leave a Mixed Legacy," *Washington Post*, April 14, 2010.

11. Steven Greenhouse, "Service Unions To Merge in Bid For More Clout," *New York Times*, January 7, 1998.

12. Moody, *US Labor in Trouble and Transition*, 115.

13. Kris Maher, "Are Unions Relevant? SEIU's Andy Stern Thinks So," *Pittsburg Post-Gazzette*, January 22, 2007.

14. Hurd, "The Failure of Organizing, the New Unity Partnership, and the Future of the Labor Movement," 5–25, 17.

15. UNITE HERE Strategic Affairs Department, "SEIU Healthcare Organizing, A Report on Issues Related to Growth and Density," This analysis was prepared by the research department of Unite Here, which admittedly is engaged in a bitter battle with SEIU.

16. John Schmitt and Ben Zipperer, "Dropping the Ax: Illegal Firings During Union Election Campaigns, 1951-2007," Center For Economic and Policy Research, March 2009, http://www.cepr.net/documents/publications/dropping-the-ax-update-2009-03.pdf.

17. Schmitt, "Dropping the Ax," 1.

18. Robert Michael Smith, *From Blackjacks to Briefcases: A History of Commercialized Strikebreaking and Union-busting in the United States*, (Athens: Ohio University Press, 2003), 75-96.

19. Kate Bronfenbrenner, "No Holds Barred: The Intensification of Employer Opposition to Organizing," Economic Policy Institute, 2009,

2.

20. Bruce Kaufman and Julie Hotchkiss, *The Economics of Labor Markets* (Thomson Higher Education: Mason, Ohio, 2006), 565-572.

21. Sara Slinn and Richard Hurd, "Fairness and Opportunity For Choice: The Employee Free Choice Act and the Canadian Model," *Just Labour: A Canadian Journal of Work and Society* (2009): 110, www.justlabour.yorku.ca/index.php?page=toc&volume=15

22. Julius Getman, *Restoring the Power of Unions: It Takes a Movement* (New Haven: Yale University Press, 2010), 265.

23. Kate Bronfenbrenner, "No Holds Barred," 3.

24. "Labor Pact at Quebec Wal-Mart," *New York Times*, April 9, 2009, http://www.nytimes.com/2009/04/10/business/global/10mart.html

25. Gompers, *Seventy Years*, 207.

26. Dan Clawson, *The Next Upsurge, Labor and the New Social Movements* (Ithaca: ILR Press, 2003), 16.

27. Clawson, *The Next Upsurge*, 13

28. Fine, *Sit-down*, 122.

29. Henry Kraus, *Heroes of Unwritten Story: The UAW, 1934-39* (Urbana: University of Illinois Press, 1993), 264.

30. Peter Friedlander, *The Emergence of a UAW Local, 1936-1939: A Study in Class and Culture* (Pittsburgh: University of Pittsburgh Press, 1975).

31. Rick Fantasia, *Cultures of Solidarity, Consciousness, Action, and Contemporary American Workers* (Berkeley: University of California Press, 1988), 20.

32. Clyde Summers, "The First Fifty Years: Questioning the Unquestioned in Collective Labor Law," *Catholic University Law Review* 47 (1998): 791, 795.

33. Bruce Nissen, "Building a "Minority Union": The CWA Experience at NCR," *Labor Studies Journal* 25, no 4 (2001): 34-55.

34. Daniel Gross and Lynd Staughton, *Solidarity Unionism at Starbucks* (Oakland; PM Press, 2011).

35. Industrial Workers of the World, "Starbucks Baristas Win Equal Treatment for MLK Day After Three Year Union Fight," November 18, 2010, http://www.iww.org/en/node/5270

36. Martin Tolchin, "A.F.L.-C.I.O. Chief Laments State of Labor Laws, " *New York Times*, August 30, 1989, http://www.nytimes.com/1989/08/30/us/afl-cio-chief-laments-state-of-labor-laws.html?pagewanted=1?pagewanted=1.

37. Richard Brisban, *A Strike Like No Other: Law and Resistance During the Pittston Coal Strike of 1989-1990* (Baltimore: John Hopkins University Press), 129.

38. Mathew Finken, "Labor Policy and the Enervation of the Economic Strike," *University of Illinois Law Review*, 1990, 547; Becker, "Better Than a Strike."

39. Fletcher, *Solidarity Divided*, 61.

40. Fletcher, *Solidarity Divided*, 128.

41. Fletcher, *Solidarity Divided*, 61.

6. THE SYSTEM OF LABOR CONTROL

1. James Atleson, *Values and Assumptions*, 1.

2. Klare, "Judicial Deradicalizaiton," 265. Others, such as Staughton Lynd, the lawyer/activist/historian argues, "the deradicalization of the Wagner Act was brought about largely by extrajudicial forces." To these analysts, factors such as economic trends, the bureaucratization of the labor movement, or global economic factors explain the rise and fall of strike activity better than legal rules.

3. *N.L.R.B. v. Jones & Laughlin Steel Corp.*, 301 U.S. 1 (1937).

4. Klare, "Judicial Deradicalizaiton," 300.

5. Feldman, "Unions, Solidarity, and Class," 187.

6. Feldman, "Unions, Solidarity and Class," 204.

7. Brecher, *Strike!*, 94-97.

8. Brecher, *Strike!*, 69.

9. Brecher, *Strike!*, 70.

10. Thomas Kochan, Harry Katz and Robert McKersie, *The Transformation of American Industrial Relations* (New York: Basic Books, 1994), 66-67.

11. Kochan, *The Transformation of American Industrial Relations*, 49.

12. Garnell, *The Rise of Teamster Power*, 115.

13. Roger Bybee, "Globalization, Use of Temps, Destroying Middle-

Class Jobs," *Working in These Times*, December 21, 2010, http://www. inthesetimes.com/working/entry/6791/globalization_use_of_temps_ destroying_middle-class_jobs/

14. Kate Bronfenbrenner, "No Holds Barred," 2.

15. Quoted in Atleson, *Values and Assumptions*, 6-7.

16. "The Supreme Court: Limits on Labor and Management," *Time Magazine*, April 9, 1965, http://www.time.com/time/magazine/article/0,9171,898618,00.html#ixzz0eD9YpHC0

17. *Textile Workers Union v. Darlington Mfg. Co*, 380 U. S. 263 (1965).

18. James Pope, "How American Workers Lost the Right to Strike," 546.

19. Marion Crain-Mountney, "Comment: The Unenforceable Successorship Clause: A Departure From National Labor Policy," *UCLA Law Review* 30: (1983).

20. Forbath, *Law and the Shaping of the Labor Movement*, 141-142.

21. Forbath, *Law and the Shaping of the Labor Movement*, 141.

22. John A. Fitch, *The Causes of Industrial Unrest* (New York: Harper Brothers , 1924), 345.

23. Fitch, *The Causes of Industrial Unrest* , 346.

24. http://www.jacksonlewis.com/legalupdates/article.cfm?aid=1736

25. Rich Trumka, "Why Labor Law has Failed," *West Virginia Law Review* 89 (1987), 871-818.

26. Kim Moody, *Workers in a Lean World: Unions in the International Economy* (London: Verso, 1997), 37.

27. Bill Fletcher, Jr and Fernando Gapasin, *Solidarity Divided: The Crisis in Organized Labor and A New Path Toward Social Justice* (Berkeley: University of California Press, 2008), 115.

28. Jeff Gammage, "The murder that galvanized Asian American activism," *The Philadelphia Enquirer* March 5, 2010, http://www.philly.com/philly/news/homepage/86505432.html

29. Fletcher, *Solidarity Divided*, 107.

30. Kim Moody, *Workers in a Lean World*, 37.

31. Fine, *Sit-down* , 21.

32. Fine, *Sit-down*, 22.

33. Ulman, *The Rise of the National Trade Union*, 42.

34. Ulman, *The Rise of the National Trade Union* , 41.

35. Ulman, *The Rise of the National Trade Union*, 42.

36. Ulman, *The Rise of the National Trade Union*, 37.

7. THE PRINCIPLES OF LABOR RIGHTS

1. Pope, James, Peter Kellman, and Ed Bruno, "Free Labor Today", *New Labor Forum* 16, no. 2 (2007): 9-18.

2. National Rifle Association, http://home.nra.org/#/home.

3. Forbath, *Law and the Shaping of the Labor Movement*, 65.

4. Forbath, *Law and the Shaping of the Labor Movement*, 143.

5. Forbath, *Law and the Shaping of the Labor Movement*, 143.

6. Samuel Gompers, *Seventy Years of Life and Labor* (New York: E.P. Dutton, 1957), 244.

7. Gompers, *Seventy Years*, 244.

8. Forbath, *Law and the Shaping of the Labor Movement*, 142.

9. Steven Greenhouse, "In Mott's Strike, More Than Pay at Stake," *New York Times*, August 17, 2010.

10. Samuel Gompers, *Labor and the Common Welfare* (New York: E. P. Dutton, 1919), 5.

11. 15 U.S.C.S. 17

12. Gompers, *Seventy Years*, 259.

13. James Gray Pope, " Labor's Constitution of Freedom," *Yale Law Journal* 106: (1997), 941, 943.

14. Neil Chamberlain, *Sourcebook on Labor* (New York: McGraw Hill, 1964), 179.

15. Chamberlain, *Sourcebook on Labor,* 188.

16. In Re Debs, 158 U. S. 564 (1885)

17. Gompers, *Seventy Years*, 252.

18. Klare, "Judicial Deradicalization," 297.

19. Karl Marx, *Wage Labor and Capital*, 1847.

20. Lawrence B. Glickman, "Labor Theory of Value" in *Encyclopedia of Labor and Working Class History*, edited by Eric Arneson (Routledge, New York, 2007), 766.

21. Lawrence B. Glickman, "Labor Theory of Value", 766.

22. Fine, *Sit-down*, 175.

23. Hansen, "The Switch in Time," 97.

24. Pope, "Free Labor Today," 9.

25. Josiah Lambert, *If the Workers Took a Notion: The Right to Strike and American Political Development* (Ithaca: ILR Press, 2005), 96-100.

26. Josiah Lambert, *If the Workers Took a Notion*, 12.

27. Pope, "Free Labor Today," 10.

28. Fitch, *Solidarity for Sale*, 69.

29. Lichtenstein, "Taft-Hartley: A Slave-Labor Law," 783.

8. LESSONS FROM THE STRUGGLE

1. Richard Brisban, *A Strike Like No Other: Law and Resistance During the Pittston Coal Strike of 1989-1990* (Baltimore: John Hopkins University Press), 199.

2. Brisban, *A Strike Like No Other*, 199-200.

3. Jim Green, "Camp Solidarity".

4. Brisban, *A Strike Like No Other*, 194.

5. "Miners' Contract Highlights," *New York Times*, February 21, 1990.

6. Suzan Erem and E. Paul Durrenberger, *On the Global Waterfront: The Fight to Free the Charleston* (New York: Monthly Review Press, 2008), 5.

7. Kari Lyderson, *Revolt at Goose Island, The Chicago Factor Takeover, and What it Says About the Economic Crisis* (Brooklyn: Melville House, 2009).

8. "Republic Windows CEO Arrested for Crimes in Looting and Closing Plant," UE News Update, September 10, 2009, http://www.ueunion.org/uenewsupdates.html?news=494

9. Lyderson, *Revolt at Goose Island*, 44-46.

10. "New! A UE Video on the Inspiring Fight by UE Members at Republic Windows and Doors," UE Union, http://www.ueunion.org/php/uewebprn.php?wsfn=ue_republic.html

11. Rachleff, *Hard-Pressed in the Heartland*; Hage, Dave and Paul Klauda, *No Retreat, No Surrender: Labor's War at Hormel* (New York: William Morrow and Co., 1989).

12. Daniel Calamuci, "Return to the Jungle: The Rise and Fall of Meatpacking Work," *New Labor Forum* 17, no. 1 (2008): 67.

13. Roger Horowitz, *Negro and White, Unite and Flight: A Social History of Industrial Unionism in Meatpacking, 1930-1990* (Urbana: University of Illinois Press, 1997).

14. Calamuci, "Return to the Jungle," 68.

15. Steven K. Ashby and C. J. Hawking Staley, *The Fight for a New American Labor Movement* (University of Illinois Press, 2009), 218.

16. Hage, *No Retreat*, 302-03.

17. Charles Craypo, *The Economics of Collective Bargaining: Case Studies in the Private Sector* (Washington, D.C.: BNA Books, 1986), 226.

18. Rachleff, *Hard-Pressed in the Heartland*, 111.

19. Ashby and Staley, *The Fight for a New American Labor Movement*, 294.

20. Ashby and Staley, *The Fight for a New American Labor Movement*, 295.

21. Getman, Julius, *Restoring the Power of Unions: It Takes a Movement* (New Haven: Yale University Press, 2010), 130.

22. Getman, *Restoring the Power of Unions*, 325.

23. "About Local 2," One Day Longer...SF, http://www.onedaylongersf. org/?page_id=2

24. Uetricht, Micah, "Around Country, UNITE-HERE Actions Take on Hotel Giant," *In These Times*, July 23, 2010, http://www.inthesitimes. com/working/entry/6259/around_country_unite-here_actions_take_ on_hotel_giant/.

25. Eugene V. Debs, "The Ideal Labor Press," *The Metal Worker*, May 1904, http://www.marxists.org/archive/debs/works/1904/laborpress. htm

9. WHERE DO WE GO FROM HERE?

1. Steven Lerner, "An Injury to All, Going Beyond Collective Bargaining as We Have Known It," *New Labor Forum* 19, no.2 (2010): 45-52.

2. Early, *Embedded with Organized Labor*, 258.

3. Henry Kraus, *Heroes of Unwritten Story*, 278.

4. Lichtenstin, *State of the Union*, 273-74.

5. Rachleff, "Is the Strike Dead?," 92.

6. 29 USCS 301-303; Higgens, *The Developing Labor Law*, 1847–1856.

7. 29 USCS 301

8. International Union, United Mine Workers of America, et. al. v. Bagwell et. al., 512 US 821, (1994).

9. Ashby and Staley, *The Fight for a New American Labor Movement*, 177.

10. Steven Lerner, "Reviving Unions," *Boston Review* (April/May, 1996), http://www.bostonreview.net/BR21.2/lerner.html.

11. American Federation of Teachers, "Joining Voices: Inclusive Strategies for Labor's Renewal," American Teacher (February 2005), http://www.aflcio.org/aboutus/ourfuture/upload/aft.pdf.

12. Janice Fine, *Workers Centers: Organizing Communities at the Edge of the American Dream* (Ithaca: ILR Press, 2006), 3.

13. Fine, *Workers Centers*, 254-55.

14. Clawson, *The Next Upsurge*.

15. Randal Archibold, "Immigrants Take to U.S. Streets in Show of Strength," *New York Times*, May 2, 2006

16. Hedges, Chris, *Death of the Liberal Class* (New York: Nation Books, 2010.)